# THE
# *RIPPLE*
# *EFFECT*

# THE *RIPPLE EFFECT*

## NETWORKING FOR *SUCCESS*

EDITED BY
·DAVID TSUBOUCHI
& MARC KEALEY

Copyright © David Tsubouchi and Marc Kealey, 2025

Published by ECW Press
665 Gerrard Street East
Toronto, Ontario, Canada M4M 1Y2
416-694-3348 / info@ecwpress.com

All rights reserved. No part of this publication may be reproduced, stored in a retrieval system, or transmitted in any form by any process — electronic, mechanical, photocopying, recording, or otherwise — without the prior written permission of the copyright owners and ECW Press. The scanning, uploading, and distribution of this book via the internet or via any other means without the permission of the publisher is illegal and punishable by law. This book may not be used for text and data mining, AI training, and similar technologies. Please purchase only authorized electronic editions, and do not participate in or encourage electronic piracy of copyrighted materials. Your support of the author's rights is appreciated.

Copy editor: David Marsh
Cover design: Jessica Albert

LIBRARY AND ARCHIVES CANADA CATALOGUING IN PUBLICATION

Title: The ripple effect : networking for success / David Tsubouchi & Marc Kealey, editors.

Other titles: Ripple effect (2025)

Names: Tsubouchi, David, editor. | Kealey, Marc, editor.

Identifiers: Canadiana (print) 20250140713 | Canadiana (ebook) 20250140721

ISBN 978-1-77041-832-5 (softcover)
ISBN 978-1-77852-412-7 (ePub)
ISBN 978-1-77852-413-4 (PDF)

Subjects: LCSH: Business networks. | LCSH: Success in business.

Classification: LCC HD69.S8 R57 2025 | DDC 650.1/3—dc23

This book is funded in part by the Government of Canada. *Ce livre est financé en partie par le gouvernement du Canada.* We also acknowledge the support of the Government of Ontario through the Ontario Book Publishing Tax Credit, and through Ontario Creates.

PRINTED AND BOUND IN CANADA

PRINTING: MARQUIS   5   4   3   2

Purchase the print edition and receive the ebook free.
For details, go to ecwpress.com/ebook.

# CONTENTS

**Foreword**    1
Dr. Michael Hartmann

**Introduction**    5
David Tsubouchi

**Meeting Random People: Networking 101**    12
Frank Gerencser

**The Valuable Asset of Social Capital: Investing in Your Network**    20
Gary Kalaci

**Networking as an Introvert**    32
David Lindsay

**The People on the Bus**    40
Shelagh Paul

**Curious, Grateful, and People-First: Networking for Future Leaders**    50
Baron Manett

**Be a Giver, Not a Taker**    58
David Tsubouchi

**An Odd Couple and the Value of Networking** 71
Marc Kealey

**No One Can Whistle a Symphony – It Takes an Orchestra** 82
Rita Davies

**Networking vs. Volunteering** 91
Rita Smith

**The Joy of Networking** 100
Susan Murray

**Why a Non-Linear Path to Networking?** 106
Stephen Brickell

**The Power of Networking: A Personal Journey** 126
Murray Simser

**Transitioning** 136
Helen Hayward

**The Power of Friendship Through Culture** 147
Chris Hope

**The Power of Meaningful Networking** 157
Anna Paluzzi

**The Entrepreneurial Journey: From NFQ to Networking** 163
Yung Wu

**Key Factors in Effective Networking** 174
Shawn Allen

**Invite Others to the Table and Ask Yourself, "What's Stopping You?"** 183
Mitzie Hunter

**What Is the Endgame of Networking? Rediscovering the Value** 193
**of Human Connection**
Krishan Mehta

**The Final Word: The Ripple Effect of Networking** 201
David Tsubouchi and Marc Kealey

# FOREWORD

## Dr. Michael Hartmann

I remember getting a call from David Tsubouchi somewhat out of the blue (which is not out of character to those with the good fortune to know him) asking if I would consider writing the foreword for his latest book — a book on networking. His choice of topic surprised me initially, as I had imagined one day writing the definitive academic textbook on the subject. Still, our conversation quickly convinced me that his version would make for a far more interesting read. We spoke for nearly an hour, reviewing possible book themes, listing potential content contributors, and comparing networking notes. A year later, I received an email with a first draft of the book and was amazed at how he could bring together such a fantastic mix of contributors so quickly. The answer, of course, quickly became apparent — David is not an academic theorist but a seasoned practitioner and consummate networker. He is also a master storyteller who creates space for diverse voices to enrich and amplify a conversation, or in this case multiple conversations, that weave together around a common theme: how to improve your networks.

As David's co-authors point out, each in their unique style, networks can transcend bureaucratic barriers, unite people around a shared purpose, unveil unforeseen opportunities, foster new relationships, and more.

Whether you're an entrepreneur seeking capital, a fresh graduate on the job hunt, or an aspiring board director looking for a new challenge, networking is the key to unlocking value in your journey. It's not just a tool; it's a powerful resource that can transform your professional life.

My thirty-plus years as a business educator have taught me that the key to effective networking is part science and part art. We can draw on powerful analytical tools to map the complex interlinkages that exist within a given network, or put more simply, help us pinpoint key network influencers and connectors. The "art" lies in navigating this web of relationships without an organizational chart, for example, knowing how and when to move from point A to point D, bypassing B and C along the way.

I have had the great fortune to talk with executives and board directors from every profession and industry. These conversations have taught me that while context and language, particularly acronyms, can vary widely across groups, we can all relate to a set of universal themes about people and relationships — stories about our family, friends, co-workers, and clients; personal triumphs and professional disappointments; and of course stories about our pets! Being a good networker does not require being a great storyteller (although it can help), but it does require you to be a great listener — to listen for points of connection. Personal connection points can build trust between people, and trust is the fuel that powers any healthy and stable network. This should come as some comfort to the introverts out there who have sharpened their listening skills. Somewhat less comforting for an introvert is that effective networking requires stepping out of your comfort zone to share details and ask questions.

———

David and Marc's book is full of insightful stories on how to grow your networks: stories for networking introverts, stories about risk-taking and saying "yes" to new connections, and stories about using networks for mentoring young people and future leaders. As an educator,

I also see the power of diverse networks in helping us challenge and broaden our perspectives. I am the current principal of the Directors College — Canada's founding professional development program for board directors. The college recently celebrated its twentieth anniversary, and an alum asked me if I stay energized after all these years teaching the same topics. I answered that while the subjects remain relatively constant, the faces in the classroom are constantly changing. To be an effective networker, be curious and reach out to the known connectors and critical influencers, but also cultivate the fringes of your networks because they can open you to lots of new opportunities and fresh perspectives.

**Dr. Michael Hartmann** is a jointly appointed professor of medicine and management at McMaster University, co-director of the university's Health Leadership Academy, and principal of the Directors College, teaching innovation governance and strategic decision-making courses. He also serves as the founding executive director of an EMBA program in digital transformation, teaching courses on corporate innovation and digital entrepreneurship with a focus on business modelling.

Michael has over twenty-five years of experience as an educational consultant, facilitator, and keynote speaker for organizations worldwide. He previously served as deputy dean and CXO at the Manchester Business School and assistant dean at the Rotman School of Management, where he established a globally ranked executive education centre. He is also the founder and principal of the educational consultancy the Leadership Portfolio and host of the *Collaboratorium Podcast Series*.

# INTRODUCTION

### David Tsubouchi

We've all heard the expression "politics makes strange bedfellows." The phrase actually originated with Shakespeare: "Misery acquaints a man with strange bedfellows." This line is spoken by Trinculo in *The Tempest*, which was published in 1610.

Back in the late 1980s, when I first entered the world of politics, I was told that it was a contact sport and no place for the meek of heart. I had never had an interest in politics when I was young because that was reserved for the elite. You had to have gone to the "best" schools and associated with the "best" people. You had to have money, and you had to be white. It was extremely rare for a member of any visible minority to hold elected office in Canada. I can remember only one at that time: Ying Hope, a prominent Chinese Canadian who was a member of Toronto's city council.

There were not a lot of visible minorities in Canada when I grew up in the 1950s and '60s. Most of us were just scrambling to earn a living and survive. The possibility of being able to hold elected office was at best remote and realistically not possible.

I was never active as a young Conservative or Liberal. I was too busy trying to earn enough money to buy a cheap car and earn my tuition. I only got involved when I was in Grade 13 and the provincial government announced they were going to extend the school year by a week. I got involved in a protest at Queen's Park to confront the minister of education, Bill Davis. My interest was not political. I just needed that week to earn enough money to pay my tuition. The government was interfering with my ability to go to school.

Later, when I was a cabinet minister and related the story to Bill Davis, by then a former premier, he chuckled and said, "David, sometimes the biggest rebels become conservatives."

I only got involved in politics when I was conscripted by ratepayers to run for a ward councillor's position in Markham. Reluctantly, I ran and won. I found that politics opened many doors and was another step in learning how to network.

Politics is, indeed, a contact sport. It is a daily thrust and parry with other political parties, and there is also the subterfuge encountered when dealing within your own political party. At least in those days, there was still some respect and camaraderie. The trick was to identify those in all parties who were sincere and had integrity. I have friends today from all parties. There are also those that require me to keep a ten-foot pole handy.

———

So how did a former Progressive Conservative cabinet minister get involved with writing a book on networking with a big-time Liberal organizer who once served as senior adviser to then–prime minister John Turner?

When I was down at Queen's Park for a visit, I was approached by Marc Kealey, who reminded me of how we had met. After this short chat, we agreed to get together.

Marc was very close to John Turner and an informal aide-de-camp for him later in life. They were inseparable. When Marc was in charge of Mr. Turner's book launch at the Economic Club in Toronto, he asked me to buy a table. I couldn't say no but I did say to Marc, "I bet

I'll be the only Conservative there." Marc just smiled and said, "Don't worry about it."

What he meant was that he had placed me at the head table with John Turner and every Liberal cabinet minister. Steve Paikin of TVOntario approached me with a puzzled look on his face. I knew what he was thinking: "Why are you sitting there?" I said jokingly to Steve, "I have pull." Then I pointed to Marc.

When Marc and I met, we realized we had a lot in common and could help each other out. Marc has since joined me in some international projects. We have travelled together and have become close friends. Marc has always supported all the community and charitable work that I do. We share different perspectives on some issues but normally we are on the same page. Marc is what I call a central hub of connections and, like me, has friends in all the political parties. I thought his perspective on networking would provide invaluable insights, considering how successful he has been.

We are the perfect example of taking a chance to get to know someone.

## WHY WE TOOK ON THIS PROJECT

Every year I lecture on diversity and, specifically, on the experience of the Japanese Canadian community during and after the wholesale imprisonment of every man, woman, and child of Japanese descent during the Second World War. My friend Dr. Merle Jacobs of the Department of Equity Studies, York University, has invited me to lecture and has made my memoir, *Gambatte*, a part of the course. I thoroughly enjoy the opportunity to share my thoughts with young, inquiring minds.

After the lectures, a dozen or so students usually approach me with additional questions. After hearing the story of how every Japanese Canadian family, including my own, was impoverished by the Canadian government, many of them ask me how I was able to get to where I am today. There are always a few really keen students who ask me if

I might have the time to share a coffee and chat. I love people who have initiative and always say yes.

Some of these students who really connect with me will call me for advice or, more usually, to talk things through. As a result of this and other relationships over the years, I have many friends who call me their mentor. Thinking about these smart, young (and some not so young) people who I would consider mentees, it struck me that most of them are East Asian, South Asian, Black, Indigenous, and women. They are from groups who have had barriers to advancement and no access to mentors. It may have turned out this way because their situations were so similar to my experience growing up.

In 2014, I received the NAAAP 100 diversity award from the North American Association of Asian Professionals in Anaheim, California. I was only the third Canadian to receive the award. The explanation of the award read: "For more than a century, Asians have overcome obstacles to make significant contributions in both America and Canada. Their contributions have added tremendously to the success and prosperity of North America. NAAAP is a leadership development organization that provides a broad range of professional and educational services. It is only fitting, then, that NAAAP recognizes leaders who exemplify our vision and mission. NAAAP is paying tribute to these leaders by creating a NAAAP 100 Recognition Program."

I remember getting a phone call from someone saying they were calling on behalf of NAAAP. It was a strange-looking phone number. Never having heard of the organization, I was a little skeptical. In addition, I misheard the caller and thought he said NAPA and I asked him why an auto parts company was calling me. He explained that his name was Ed Hwang and that he was the president of NAAAP. Ed went on to tell me that the Toronto chapter of NAAAP had nominated me for an award called the NAAAP 100 and that they would like to fly me down to Anaheim to receive it at their annual convention.

I was a little surprised and asked him why they had chosen me. He advised me that Ben Hum, the president of the Toronto chapter, had nominated me, as I was the first Japanese Canadian to be elected as a member of a provincial legislature in Canada, and also the first cabinet minister. He also mentioned my work in diversity. I was flattered to hear this and even more so when I heard that Gary Locke, the former governor of Washington State and former Secretary of Commerce under President Barack Obama, was one of the other recipients. Locke was the first Chinese American to serve as a governor.

After the conversation I called Ben Hum, who confirmed the story. When I attended the convention, I learned that the big issue for the organization was the lack of mentors. When I accepted the award, I looked at the crowd of thousands of Asian professionals and saw that there were very few greybeards like me, and I realized how deep the issue ran. I did mention the responsibility of the older generations to share their experiences, stories, and advice with younger people.

The value of passing on one's wisdom is a realization that comes with age and experience. Someone asked me the other day why I help so many people and don't ask for anything. I asked him, what would be more satisfying: having a few thousand dollars more or helping someone succeed and knowing you had a part in it? It is not as altruistic as it sounds. Basking in someone else's success is a wonderful feeling.

———

Sometimes, the things that you can do are so small and easy to do. Many of the things that you can do are the result of having a large network and just making an introduction. Others take a longer time and commitment.

When you think about it, the reason why people are looked upon as wise is their experience and the lessons learned. In other words, we have learned a lot through our failures, and especially through our perseverance. Most of us have succeeded because we have failed, and sometimes failed spectacularly. We have survived the mistakes of our youth — and thankfully before the time of social media.

The other side of the coin, networking, is not so much a skill as an opportunity. When people ask me how they can network, they are asking how they can reach beyond their grasp. Networking is a process much like building a house. You need a strong foundation and that takes time.

As you will learn, networking requires taking yourself out of your comfort zone. Many say that the fear of death is only exceeded by the fear of giving a speech. I would add that going up to and introducing yourself to someone you do not know is probably somewhere high on that scale, especially if you are an introvert like I used to be.

In the end, networking requires time and determination. Mentoring requires time and attitude. Finding a mentor requires time and courage. And we all have a limited amount of time. In the end, mentoring expands the networks of both mentors and mentees. All of the contributors to this book also happen to be very generous mentors, as networking and mentoring are both two-way streets.

## WHAT'S IN THIS BOOK

I have always loved good stories. I love authors who can weave an interesting tale and at the same time have a point to what they are writing. I have taken the same approach to giving speeches. I love telling stories.

There's nothing worse than sitting and listening to someone who drones on and on with a million statistics while you sit there wondering whether you are in some existentialist play. The best speakers make their point through stories. I have had the pleasure of listening many times to former prime minister Brian Mulroney, who I consider to have been one of the most interesting speakers; he succeeded in making his point through personal experiences and self-deprecating tales. Similarly, John Turner had some rip-roaring stories that made me cry from laughter.

So instead of just telling you how to network, we decided to *illustrate* how through a series of short stories and vignettes and what you might consider postings. Marc and I decided that the best way to write about networking was to get successful networkers to write about their experiences and the lessons they have learned. We decided to tap our combined networks and asked our friends who happen to come from different backgrounds — ethnic, economic, business and marketing, politics and government, education, law, and entertainment — if they would contribute. And they said yes.

We hope you will gain some ideas on how to improve your network. I just like meeting interesting people, but as a friend of mine once said: A better network equals better net worth.

# MEETING RANDOM PEOPLE: NETWORKING 101

### Frank Gerencser | Founder of triOS College

In November 2016, I was sitting in the back of a conference room in Toronto listening to speakers at the Conference Board of Canada's fourth Skills and Post-Secondary Education Summit. The speakers and attendees were a who's who of Canada's public post-secondary education (PSE) sector, including administrators (presidents, provosts, and directors), educators (chairs, deans, and professors), and other interested parties (members of Provincial Parliament [MPPs], members of the Legislative Assembly [MLAs], researchers, and Indigenous representatives).

My wife would often ask me why I was going to an event like this. I'd tell her it was "to meet random people and create random opportunities," which I always did. Of course, everyone going to this event was adjacent to my circle in post-secondary education, so I was going to the right place at the right time.

I think I was the only private career college (PCC) participant in the audience. At the time, I owned a dozen career college campuses from Windsor to Halifax, training domestic students for new careers in business, technology, and healthcare.

There is a pecking order of prestige in PSE: Research universities are at the top, followed by teaching universities, larger then smaller community colleges, apprenticeship training, and finally career colleges.

We were one of the largest career college groups in Ontario, and as a former chair of both Career Colleges Ontario and the National Association of Career Colleges, I had a different perspective than our public peers.

Our students are different — they average thirty-three years old but range from eighteen to sixty-eight or older, as opposed to typical public PSE students, who average twenty-two years old and range from seventeen to twenty-five. Our students' prior education spans degrees, diplomas, and high school. They are less concerned about getting a higher education credential than getting a fast, focused education leading to a job.

This brings me back to the conference. The plenary session before lunch was Ensuring Successful Transition from Secondary to Post-Secondary Education. The speaker panel included MPP Peggy Sattler (then the NDP education critic), Steven Coté (director of policy for the Canada Student Loans program), and the Hon. David H. Tsubouchi (then registrar and CEO of the Ontario College of Trades).

I listened to the speakers, and as usual, the focus was on preparing secondary students for public post-secondary education. The only way to get anyone to comment on the value of training at career colleges was to ask a specific question. This is also the best way to get people to know who you are.

There were two microphones on stands in the aisles at the back of the room. As the session ended, the audience was invited to ask questions of the panel. I *always* ask questions, especially as, in an event with over five hundred people in the room, only a handful of them would get a chance to ask. My preference is to ask the second question so that the first one breaks the ice.

I addressed the panel, briefly introducing myself and triOS College, then directing my question to David. I asked how secondary students could learn about the "third pillar of PSE, career colleges." I don't remember what he said, as my objective in asking the question was so that I could do a follow-up and make an introduction after the session concluded.

The plenary broke for lunch, and I walked up to the platform to introduce myself to David. There were a few others asking questions, and I waited until I'd be the last one before he left. I thanked him for his presentation and his answer to my question.

I talked a bit more about our PCC sector and suggested we could have a coffee together to discuss this further. He agreed and we exchanged cards.

The next part is important — follow up! I did, and after the usual back and forth between my staff and his, we agreed that I would come to his office for a coffee in late January 2017. I brought a little bit of marketing material on our college, but this wasn't so much a sales pitch as a chance to meet and connect for future opportunities.

It was a friendly meeting — if you know David, you know that's just how he is, a friendly guy. I asked if he'd ever visited a private career college, which he hadn't. I suggested that he visit our Toronto campus, which ultimately happened in June 2017.

This is another part of my networking strategy: Make the person you want to build a relationship with invest time with you, in this case by commuting to a meeting, taking a tour, and talking to some of our staff and students. He came away from the meeting with a new understanding, and we both felt positive about each other.

This led to an October 2017 meeting in our Campus Support Centre in Mississauga to discuss the possibility of David joining triOS's corporate Board of Advisors. Participating in the Board of Advisors is an easier ask than joining a board of directors, as they don't have any fiduciary duty — they're "just" listening and giving advice.

In March 2018, David joined our board as the political adviser and has been with us ever since.

So, what value did we get from the relationship? Well, it seems that David knows everyone (or at least a few thousand influencers in government and higher education). He is well regarded as a red Conservative or blue Liberal, reaching out on both sides of the aisle.

He is also on many boards and involved with many associations and is happy to make introductions to them.

In January 2020, mere weeks before COVID-19 shut down the province, we launched a public-private partnership with Sault College to train international students in Brampton and part of Toronto for new careers in business, technology, and healthcare. A year later, we signed an agreement with Mohawk College to train international students in Mississauga.

Both partnerships started with training students online because of COVID restrictions. But we needed to find or build a location to teach in person. The best possible location in Mississauga was in Square One Shopping Centre, the largest mall in Ontario. We had a triOS College campus on the ring road surrounding it for over twenty years, but felt that being right in the mall would be ideal.

Square One is the epicentre of Mississauga, housing the main transit terminal and soon the centre of the LRT, the new light rapid transit line being built through Mississauga and Brampton. However, they'd never had a school operating inside the mall. COVID changed everything — mall attendance and subsequently tenant occupancy suffered, and they needed to consider alternative uses.

I approached David for his help, as he was on the board of the Ontario Municipal Employees' Retirement System (OMERS), which owns Oxford Properties, which in turn owns Square One. David simply broached the idea with the CEO of OMERS, who put in a call to the CEO of Oxford (neither of whom I'd met yet), who connected me to the head of retail for Canada, Bradley Jones. The two of us hit it off right away. By coincidence, his wife grew up in the house directly across the street from ours in Burlington — a small world indeed.

Square One had a 58,000-square-foot space from a former Home Outfitters and Dollarama that had been vacant for over five years. Most of it was gutted — all it had was concrete columns and fifteen-foot-high ceilings.

I pitched Brad on the value to their food courts of bringing 3,500 hungry bellies to school every day. These international students would also buy from and work for stores in the mall. They would typically be aged twenty-three to twenty-five and already have a degree from their home countries. Their goal was to qualify for a post-secondary work permit and ultimately Canadian citizenship.

Fast forward to fall 2023, when we signed a long-term agreement, designed the space in three phases, moved in, expanded, and expanded again, and had a pair of ribbon cuttings with the mayor and Brad from Oxford attending. It's worked wonderfully for all involved.

Along the way, Sault College was looking for more space. So we signed an agreement with Oxford for 55,000 square feet in the Scarborough Town Centre, which would go live in two phases, in September 2024 and 2025. Unfortunately, the federal immigration ministry introduced a new policy in January 2024 that blocked this expansion before construction started.

From start to finish: I attended an event just to make connections in 2016 that resulted in David joining our advisory board and opening doors to Square One and Scarborough Town Centre, and ultimately over 7,000 students studying with us. That's a lot of downstream value from attending a random networking event to meet random people to drive random opportunities.

You never know where a networking connection will take you. Most go nowhere, but like a golf game (for me anyhow), every once in a while you get that great drive that keeps you coming back for more.

———

I've had many other trails of networking connections that I won't take up your time with. But here's a snapshot of a chain of events that ultimately spawned our career training division (before we officially became triOS College).

My first company after graduating from the University of Waterloo in systems design engineering was called Architech Microsystems. A classmate and I started it in 1984 as a systems integrator, buying computer components from Canadian distributors and assembling complete solutions for individuals and companies.

We built a good name and had a strong relationship with our suppliers. One night in the late '80s, I got a call from a teacher at Westwood Secondary named Ron Maruya (in 2023, he was a principal in the Halton school district). He needed a printer ribbon for a Roland printer that he had. He called the distributor, Amdahl, and they gave Ron my name. What he needed was just a $10 part, but he was desperate, so I agreed to stay late for him to pick up the one I had in stock.

Ron and I hit it off immediately and he said I needed to meet Gary Hollo, one of his peers, who'd moved to the Peel school district and ran part of their continuing education division. I called Gary and he agreed to meet. At the time, my office was mere blocks away. Gary met me at Tapster's Bar and Grill along with a couple of his peers. He explained they were offering career training programs funded by Human Resources Development Canada (HRDC) and needed to buy a couple of dozen computers at a time. Over the next several years, we supplied them with over three hundred computers and related networking and printing equipment.

I had split with my first business partner in March 1993, and a year later Gary called me up to see how I was doing. The long and short of it was that we did a joint venture of triOS Training Centres with the Peel District School Board to train unemployed people to become networking technicians known as advanced certified engineers for SCO UNIX operating systems. The training was fully funded by HRDC, and we did a great job for them, with 100 percent graduating and getting a related IT job. HRDC said do it again . . . and again and again. We built a whole business on this, first in Mississauga, then Toronto. Altogether, we trained about three hundred students.

It was a successful partnership until it wasn't — one day we got a call from HRDC saying they were out of the direct funding business. We pivoted, launched a novel "Job Offer Guarantee Program," and explored acquiring a private career college registration to get access to stable funding through the Ontario Student Assistance Program. We learned about a bankrupt, five-campus school chain and agreed to buy it (sight unseen) in an hour-long call with the superintendent just before the Labour Day weekend in 1998, and we became a registered private career college — triOS College of Information Technology.

Skipping decades of growth, challenges, and acquisitions, we've now graduated over eighty thousand people into careers in business, technology, and healthcare. Not bad for a printer ribbon lead that I treated with the same care I would with anyone spending a lot more money with us.

———

The lesson to take away from this is you never know where a networking event will lead. The more often you participate in random (though targeted) events, the more connections you will make, *if* you follow them up. You don't need to know where they will lead — they always lead somewhere, and once in a while to a very good place.

I'm ethnically Hungarian by descent, though born in Sudbury, Ontario. After working and taking over the family paint and aluminum business after my father passed when I was twelve years old — and learning that we had a mortgage (most kids that age don't know what they are) and owed suppliers significant amounts of money — I would ask my mother how we were going to survive. She answered "Majd lesz valahogy," which translates to "somehow it will all work out." It's been my guiding north star all my life.

Applying this to networking, keep on making connections. Figure out how you can help them solve their problems and it will result in opportunities for you somehow. From microphone questions to gorgeous campuses, from printer ribbons to whole new businesses, there is a world of opportunities available to you. All you need to do is reach out and start — "Hi, my name is Frank. I'm pleased to meet you."

**Frank Gerencser** is the founder of triOS College, the largest private college group in Canada. Born and raised above his mother's Hungarian restaurant, Frank was introduced to the world of business early on, helping in his father's paint and aluminum business from the age of nine. After his father's death, he took charge of the family business as a teenager, where he developed his skills in sales, installations, and customer service.

In addition to co-founding triOS College, Frank also acquired Eastern College in the Maritimes and several other colleges and grew the combined business to sixteen campuses, over eighty thousand graduates, ten thousand full-time students, and nine hundred employees.

# THE VALUABLE ASSET OF SOCIAL CAPITAL: INVESTING IN YOUR NETWORK

### Gary Kalaci | Founder and CEO of Alexa Translations

In the fast-paced business world, where financial capital influences many decisions, the true power lies in an often underestimated asset: social capital. While financial capital has economic force, social capital provides stability. Harnessing the transformative power of social capital can expand your potential and help you build a thriving business.

Social capital is the combined practical benefits of social networks, relationships, and interactions. It is based on mutual interests and enables groups to work together effectively towards a shared goal. Social capital sets a thriving business, career, and personal growth apart from a stagnant one. Likewise, the quality of your social relationships is a crucial factor influencing your happiness and, as a result, impacts your overall well-being.

The three forms of social capital are bonding, bridging, and linking. Bonding refers to social capital created within a group with shared interests and goals. Commonly found within your team and workplace, bonding is about your internal social circle. Bridging, on the other hand, means creating new relationships beyond your current circle. Networking with other entrepreneurs is an example of how bridging works. Linking, similar to bridging, builds relationships between people at different hierarchical levels. For example, when the CEO of a company meets with the staff and learns about their daily routines, they can develop more efficient work practices. The lower-level staff can also build connections with higher-level staff, which serves as a vertical bridge.

## OPENING THE DOOR TO A NEW OPPORTUNITY

New opportunities will find those who open the right doors. Social capital creates opportunities for gaining knowledge, resources, and experience through leveraging networks and relationships with the right people. This is precisely why building social capital is more complex than financial capital.

One of the biggest challenges in a career or new business is access. Access means finding the right contacts to advance your career or become potential customers. Opening doors was critical in the few years after starting my company, so I focused on building a suitable client base, using relationships I established in university. In addition, meeting new people through networking events supercharged my early days of network development. As my career progressed, it became more difficult. Between running a small business and having a family to look after, there was a lot to juggle, and it took a lot of work to achieve the right balance. However, I knew this was critical for advancement.

Social capital acted as a catalyst for growth and opened the door for business. Financial resources were typically more limited in the early days, so my initial efforts in building social capital facilitated much of the early growth of my business. Although it is difficult, you need to invest enough time to develop the core building blocks of social capital. Stay disciplined in building your brand, get your name out there, and connect with as many people as possible.

## THE VALUE OF ENDURING RELATIONSHIPS

Later in one's career, social capital can be equally handy, especially when times get tough. As the COVID-19 pandemic disrupted many industries, our business, like many others, was thrown into uncharted territory. The sudden lockdowns and shifting consumer behaviour created a period of uncertainty. With this abrupt change in the business, adjustments became imperative.

The inability to conduct face-to-face meetings, attend industry events, or engage in the usual networking activities hindered traditional business development methods. Departments were realigned, remote work became the norm, and digitalization accelerated. However, in this time of uncertainty, I found solace in my existing network. The relationships cultivated over the years became an invaluable asset. Existing clients, partners, and stakeholders provided steady support, offering a semblance of stability during turbulent times.

My team and I continued to nurture and strengthen the existing relationships at our company. Client retention and satisfaction became more vital than ever. Partnerships and trust built over the years became a beacon of hope. We explored creative ways to engage with our existing network — virtual events, online workshops, and tailored solutions to address clients' unique challenges. Amid struggles, our team found that enduring the storm meant embracing change and relentlessly pursuing innovation. Unlike many companies facing the pandemic, we thrived in this time of hardship because of our investments in social capital. Even after the pandemic, these investments highlight the continuous effort and consistent cultivation required to develop adequate social capital.

## HOW TO BUILD SOCIAL CAPITAL IN PRACTICE

Building social capital requires patience, strategic planning, and a long-term perspective, much like financial investments. Throughout your deliberate and consistent efforts to contribute knowledge, nurture connections, and cultivate trust, you also must understand that the returns may not always be immediate.

You must consistently make "deposits" through regular touchpoints to build adequate social capital. You need to develop your brand and showcase your efforts constantly. It isn't about showing off and saying, "Look at all these things I'm involved in," but these initiatives reinforce your name in people's minds, building your reputation and relevancy.

There will be many situations where people in your network need help to advance their careers, identify new clients, or look for a new job opportunity. These are some of the more critical times for you to add value. It is a lot of work, but it is also the time to be the most proactive in your efforts.

Anyone can accomplish this, and in different ways. You can connect over coffee, lunch, or dinner. Also, notably, these touchpoints don't have to be limited to in-person interactions. Virtual catchups through email, LinkedIn, text messaging, or even calls are great ways to dedicate time to your social network consistently. You will also want to find the right timing. Celebrating essential milestone achievements, attending landmark events, sending out holiday or birthday wishes, or even sending gifts are great examples of *when* to engage with your social connections.

## START NETWORKING

Networking is the core building block in developing social capital. In the beginning, it can be intimidating to get out of your comfort zone and network, but all entrepreneurs must take risks. Like anything in life, you will refine your networking skills through practice and iteration. Do not be afraid to reach out to people in your network for introductions, find like-minded people to attend networking events with, and volunteer at non-profit initiatives or industry events.

While networking can be daunting for some, one relatively easy thing you can control is to make yourself presentable. It's always better to arrive at events overdressed rather than underdressed, as the first impression is often critical. At a glance, you want to show people that you *belong* there.

Social capital is ultimately built upon a human instinct, which asks, "Can I trust this person?" With that in mind, I advise against approaching someone and pitching your business too early. They are less likely to open up to you if you make the interaction too transactional. This makes them feel like they are being commoditized and builds a barrier to wanting to do business. The goal is to develop a meaningful relationship. Ask questions to build trust and rapport. Get to know them — what their interests are, what family they have, what they like to do outside of work. I recommend against bringing up what you do for work *at all*. If you talk about what *they* do for work, they will almost always ask what you do afterward.

Also, quality trumps quantity. Do not try to meet as many people as possible; it's not a numbers game. You are always better off establishing two to five quality connections rather than fifteen to twenty surface-level ones. Remember, your goal is to build trust through a genuine conversation. Ask them the right questions and establish a solid connection. Then they will be more likely to accept an invitation to touch base later, turning this into a long-term relationship and potentially a business opportunity.

Many people you meet might not become customers directly, but they can sometimes provide referrals, become brand ambassadors, or simply be part of your ecosystem in the marketplace. Always approach networking with confidence, but do not pretend like you know it all. It is vital to have the humility to ask questions and take the time early on to network and learn as much as you can. Time is a commodity you have less of later on in your career, so utilize it as effectively as possible.

## IDENTIFY RECRUITMENT OPPORTUNITIES

How you connect with people can also bring different types of opportunities to light. You can build your social worth through potential business opportunities, but you also might find several talented individuals perfect for your team, should you be in a hiring position. Your team is a reflection of yourself, so having the right people is crucial. Being able to find like-minded individuals and get them to buy into a shared vision can be a difficult task. While networking, you can identify opportunities to recruit some of the individuals you connect with. Investing in social capital requires effort into team building, collaboration, and shared values.

I initially met my vice-president of marketing at a marketing conference, and we became acquainted because we kept running into each other at various events throughout the year. At the time, I had no idea he would one day join our organization, but his name immediately came to mind when we were looking to expand our executive team. Likewise, our current head of product is someone I used to work with as a client, and we have kept in regular touch. So, when the time was right, and there was a fit within our organization, we reconnected and added him to our team. Keeping an eye out for these connections can add meaningful value to your organization.

Ultimately, you want to invest the time to understand who you align with and how you can benefit jointly with them. Doing so effectively "diversifies your portfolio" by opening up different value points, whether they're recruitment opportunities or other benefits of networking.

## SEEK OUT MENTORS

In business, separating yourself from your ego is essential as it can hinder your growth as an entrepreneur. The more you learn from mentors and industry leaders in the early stages, the better. You can learn a wealth of knowledge from mentorship. Having access to this resource is well-suited to building your social capital.

I encourage everyone to seek mentorship early in their career and, further, to get mentors for all aspects of life — social, personal, and professional. This is low-hanging fruit and a great way to absorb some valuable information. If you're intimidated to reach out, don't be. Most are surprised by how often these accomplished individuals will take on a mentorship role. They were once in a similar position in their career. Remember to always be prepared to learn and be respectful of their time.

At a Canadian marketing conference, one of the speakers I was interested in was an executive vice-president of a large loyalty company. After I saw her speak at the event, I reached out to her on LinkedIn and introduced myself. I said, "It was impressive to hear you speak at the conference. I'd love to connect with you and learn more about what you're doing." She replied, "Thank you for reaching out, but we are not interested in professional translation services." I immediately changed the conversation's trajectory by saying, "I completely understand, but the reason I reached out wasn't about selling you my product but rather to see what I can learn from you." As a result, we met for coffee and have stayed in touch ever since. Her business advice has been beneficial. In fact, in time, we ended up doing business together, and to this day, we still collaborate in several ways.

Every dollar matters in the formative times of your business, but you still need to be disciplined about not making interactions transactional. Learning as much as possible is essential. Business will always come if you invest your time correctly.

## CHOOSE THE RIGHT LOCATIONS

*Where* you network is just as important as who you connect with. With no initial investments and a limited network, my approach to building social capital was methodical. I was purposeful in choosing who to meet and where to meet them, gravitating towards suitable events, social gatherings, and organizations.

A thorough networking plan relies on consistent effort, so staying committed to being out two or three evenings a week to meet new people was a guiding principle in building my social network. When you network, you want to focus on the task at hand and develop your relationships. Making your environment predictable makes this process easier, as the only variable you need to worry about is the networking.

Ultimately, it's about making sure you know the interests of the individual you're networking with — whether it's a client or a prospect — and tailoring the event, venue, or activity to the unique interests of the individual. This personalized approach shows that you value their preferences and helps in building stronger, more genuine connections. Whether it's arranging a golf outing for a finance professional who loves the sport or organizing a private wine-tasting session for a legal expert who appreciates fine wine, tailoring your approach can make all the difference.

Similarly, I like to return to the places where I can expect excellent and predictable service. One of the places I use to host events is Jump Restaurant in Toronto. Since this establishment is so central, meeting people from every corner of the city is easy, but that's not why I continually go there. I became friends with the owner there as a young entrepreneur and made it part of my routine to dine there weekly, not only to open doors to meeting people but also to support the restaurant of a close friend. Predictability around choosing locations for lunch, dinner, or coffee will alleviate decision fatigue and make it easier for you and your support staff to schedule these meetings. Establishing these regular venues to make your personal process more predictable is worth the effort.

## GIVE MORE THAN YOU TAKE

Like any investment, the goal of building social capital is often to accrue value. However, you must invest before you can make any withdrawals. Providing insights, experience, or expertise in your area will give you a foot in the door when approaching established individuals. As an active contributor to the ecosystem, you show others that you have value, which provides you an opening with them. You leverage what you can offer as an opportunity to benefit from the exchange mutually.

Adam Grant, the author of *Give and Take: Why Helping Others Drives Our Success* (2014), highlights that strategic giving is the best way to succeed in business and in life. Giving remains invaluable in the acquisition of social capital. I always give first before asking for something in return. There is no better way to build social capital than helping those in need within your network.

However, as your business grows, so does your social responsibility. Giving *back* is equally important as it allows you to "reinvest your earnings" into the ecosystem that brought you up. The ways you can give back to your community — charitable activities, social responsibility initiatives, scholarships, and partnerships — demonstrate a commitment to community welfare while simultaneously building social capital.

I met a senior banking executive and vice-chairman of an accounting firm through one of my previous involvements with the United Way. We became lifelong friends. Once I got my business off the ground, this connection opened introductions to many senior executives in the financial, legal, and securities industries. This friendship I made early in my career created business opportunities many years later.

## BUILDING BRIDGES, NOT BARRIERS

Another way you can add value is to *facilitate* collaboration and networking between others. My social value grew as I helped people build bridges, establishing a solid network and social connections. Not only do you solidify your role as a conduit in networking, but you also reinforce the value you provide in the ecosystem. To do this effectively, you must be purposeful in making social connections.

In product marketing, a positioning canvas is a standard tool to help businesses define their orientation in the marketplace. It outlines an organization's market category, unique value proposition, competitive alternatives, and best-fit customers. You can adopt this concept into a *social* positioning canvas in networking to better understand your various connections' qualifications, skill sets, and interests and inform how you build more meaningful social relationships.

By connecting the dots, you become a conduit for productive interactions and solidify your investments in social capital. For example, by understanding that Sally is a senior accountant with over ten years of experience, specializes in trading mutual funds, and loves red wine, you can consolidate Sally's unique value propositions and match them to someone with similar interests and skills. I refer to this as the "matrix of collaboration," and it facilitates better compatibility in developing social connections. By harnessing this ideology, you evolve into a required component in the networking process, cementing your role in the social sphere.

## BECOMING A THOUGHT LEADER

The more people I connected with, the more I saw that knowledge-sharing is the foundation for building social capital. I saw so much value in hosting dinners and bringing people together to foster communication and connection. I took these as opportunities to reinvest in my social capital portfolio and provide valuable insights to those seeking them. The main focus is on learning in both the early and later stages of building social capital.

You gain value through learning from people more experienced than you, but you also solidify your reputation by educating others. Not only did I elevate myself as an entrepreneur, but I also evolved into a thought leader in my industry. I started engaging in public speaking, developed my public image, wrote articles, and became more active on social media platforms. The goal was to get my story out there and give new entrepreneurs an avenue to build themselves up, just like my early mentors did. People start to look to you for leadership and valuable insights. This is what consistent deposits in social capital can provide — a rich social network that facilitates personal and professional growth.

## KEY TAKEAWAYS

Building something out of nothing is every entrepreneur's dream but requires perseverance and resourcefulness. My journey from a newcomer in Canada to a successful entrepreneur elucidates the power of social capital. My story serves as a testament to the enduring value of social capital in fostering personal and professional growth, navigating challenges, and contributing to the broader entrepreneurial ecosystem. The commitment to give more than take reinforces that building social capital is a reciprocal and evolving process. It highlights a symbiotic relationship between knowledge-sharing and the accrual of social capital.

Be consistent in developing your social connections, always put yourself out there, be genuine, be respectful, and always pay it forward. Strive to provide valuable insights, unlock opportunities through strategic networking, seek mentorship to propel your growth, and harness the transformative power of social connections in your endeavours.

A lawyer and award-winning entrepreneur, **Gary Kalaci** is CEO of Alexa Translations, a leader in AI translation technology and services. In addition to steering the strategy and growth efforts of his translation company, Gary has held leadership positions and sat on the boards of directors at several professional associations and not-for-profit organizations. Gary's business and legal training armed him with the skills required to work with clients across the finance, corporate, legal, and government sectors, among others.

# NETWORKING AS AN INTROVERT

### David Lindsay | Chair of the Board at Infrastructure Ontario

People network in different ways and for different reasons. For some it comes naturally, but for others it takes more effort and forethought. As an introvert, I had to learn how to network. To this day, I must resist my tendency to step back. The experience is rewarding once you get going, but that first step can be the hardest. With a deliberate plan and a positive attitude, anyone can become a natural networker — even an introvert.

Networking is the act of interacting with others. How you approach the interaction can make it a rewarding experience or a dead end. A positive approach with a genuine desire for mutual benefit is much more motivating and sustaining. Approach it with that attitude. Be positive and look for mutual benefit.

Posting a photo on LinkedIn is not networking. If the post leads to a follow-up personal engagement, then you are networking. Attending a professional conference or business luncheon is not networking. Making a contact that generates deliberate follow-up is networking. Simply handing out business cards at a conference is not networking. Good networking is a two-way process. You need to engage; you need to listen and create dialogue.

## FOUR STEPS TO MEETING AND CREATING DIALOGUE

Joining a professional association, attending a regular business luncheon, or signing up for a conference all create platforms for networking. Attending a networking event is important but is only the first step. You must have a strategy to engage and make a connection. Finding a common interest doesn't always happen right away, but demonstrating your interest in the other person usually creates a positive first impression. Signalling your interest in the individual usually predisposes the other person to reciprocate.

Introverts don't like to be the ones to create dialogue, so you need to consciously decide to engage. A positive attitude and a few icebreakers will help get you started — just a few lines to open the door for further engagement.

I have attended many luncheon speeches and business conferences. When I was younger, I would go to my assigned table at the lunch and wait for the program to start. I avoided interacting with others whom I didn't already know. As I became more confident, I spent a bit more time in the lobby mixing and mingling before taking my seat. I would force myself to say hello to people. Remember: All these people came to this event for a reason. Like you, they have an interest in the subject. Don't think of them as strangers but as people with a shared interest. They want to learn from you, and you want to learn from them.

If you find a room full of people a bit daunting, then take it slowly. Focus on one or two interesting people you would like to meet. You are not trying to win over the whole room. The first step was showing up; now you are just making polite conversation.

The trick in those social settings is to find a topic that prompts conversation, creating a connection. Simply thrusting out your hand and saying, "Hello, my name is . . ." can sometimes end with an awkward silence unless you have a follow-up strategy. Be ready to engage. After you have introduced yourself, a little small talk helps break the ice.

Networking as an Introvert | 33

Sharing stories about the weather or the traffic getting to the event are usually safe starters. Asking someone if they have any vacation plans or, depending on the time of year, how they spent the holidays, or whether they saw the game last night, can all be ways to start a conversation. Have two or three of those open-ended questions ready to gently nudge a conversation along. If you hear something in the response that might create another open-ended question, follow that thread. You want to establish a bit of rapport with the individual before launching into business conversation. So if they say, "Traffic wasn't too bad," ask another open-ended question like "How far do you commute?" or "Where in the city is home?" By asking a follow-up question, you are demonstrating an interest in the person. Making a connection. As you get comfortable, the conversation should naturally turn to the business at hand. You are both at the same event; there is more often than not some mutual interest you can develop, and that is more likely to happen if you have made that human connection.

A bridge line from the casual conversation to the business at hand might be "What attracted you to come to this conference?" or "What are you hoping to hear from the speaker today?" First, you asked something to signal you are interested in them as a person; now you are seeking a mutual interest in the topic or some business interests you might share.

The conversation creates the connection, but don't put unrealistic pressure on yourself. Not every connection automatically becomes a business deal or a new sale. The connection creates an opportunity for follow-up.

Creating the opening for further engagement is the mark of a good networking encounter. So have a couple of "next-step" phrases in mind. "It was nice to meet you," without any additional phrase, sounds like you are terminating the conversation without any follow-up. If you want to build the relationship, you need a next-step phrase. "I hope to see you at the next conference" is the least aggressive. "I would like to learn more about how you got involved in this business. We should have coffee sometime" signals an interest in deepening the connection.

In summary, the four steps are: First, show up and proactively engage. Second, ask open-ended questions to demonstrate interest in the people you meet. Third, try to establish a mutual interest, and if that interest exists, step four is creating a follow-up opportunity.

―――

Developing a network of connections takes time. The more you are circulating, the more you develop your network. Once you have made the connection, an occasional follow-up is important. Like watering a house plant, you must not neglect a contact for too long. An occasional phone call or sharing of a recent article of interest is a good excuse to keep a contact alive.

Sending a note on someone's birthday is one common way to maintain contact. But you can find more creative and interesting excuses to connect. One consummate networker who maintained an impressive Rolodex was the late Peter Herrndorf. I got to know Peter when he was the head of TVOntario. Every couple of months, I would get a clipping from the *New York Times* or some other publication with a handwritten note from Peter: "Thought you might be interested." He was able to maintain connections with people with a steady stream of short notes and newspaper clippings.

Sometimes, the most interesting connections happen by accident. But with a little imagination, you can turn what might be a one-off interaction into a regular contact. Like Herrndorf's clipping strategy, sending a quick email, or leaving a voicemail message whenever something reminds you of your contact, is another way to keep the engagement going. Maybe a guest speaker at a conference you both attended was recently in the news. That's an opportunity to refresh your connection and say hello.

―――

September 11, 2001, was a terrible tragedy. Many of us remember where we were and what we were doing when we heard the news. That morning, I happened to be participating in a roundtable discussion with a group of community leaders in the Waterloo region on the subject of infrastructure investments. We were in a small boardroom when we heard the news. Every September 11, for the next decade, I would call or send a short note to each of the individuals to remind them where we were on that historic day.

Fast forward eleven years. In September 2012, I was starting a new job as head of the Forest Products Association of Canada in Ottawa. In my first week on the job, the receptionist ran into my office one morning and seemed a little rattled. "What's wrong?" I asked. "It's the Governor General's office on the phone. He wants to talk to you." I smiled and said, "Of course . . . it's September 11."

The caller was David Johnston, who was the president at the University of Waterloo in September 2001. Eleven years later, on September 11, he phoned to welcome me to Ottawa and invite me to Rideau Hall to talk about the forest products industry.

People do like to maintain contact, but it takes effort. You need a little system to remind you to keep those contacts fresh. It takes effort, but the payback is a rich reward of friends and business associates.

———

For most of my professional career, I have had a personal hobby of birdwatching. For me, it isn't a group activity. I enjoy the quiet and solitude of walking in nature, observing and studying the habits of birds. I call it my "non-people time" or my private time. I never expected that my birdwatching would help with networking.

During the COVID-19 pandemic, I started posting some of my bird pictures on social media. My solo hobby became a vehicle to create social interaction during the COVID lockdown. People who I never thought were interested in birdwatching were sending me grainy photos they had taken with their phones. "David, I saw this bird yesterday. Do you know what it is?" People I hadn't spoken with in several years were suddenly reacting to my bird photos.

It was rewarding to be able to engage with friends and colleagues during the lockdown. And I was surprised how many were appreciative of this unusual opportunity to connect. Pre-pandemic, when I would share my passion for birdwatching at the office, it usually didn't get much reaction. The conversation would quickly turn to the Blue Jays — and I don't mean birds but baseball. During COVID, my bird photography became a way to create dialogue. The long periods of lockdown created a need for that human connection, and my personal hobby was a vehicle to start an exchange and share experiences.

The human need for regular contact produces the exchange of ideas and information, so it is not just a business skill but an important part of the social makeup of each of us. A desire to connect, to validate, and to share has intrinsic benefits beyond just helping you get a job or find a new customer for your business.

Networking is about making the connection as human beings, sharing common interests, and learning and growing from the experience. Of course, making a regular point of connecting with people and cultivating relationships does build a pool of potential contacts for those business opportunities. One of my current business projects resulted from an exchange about a bird photograph on X (formerly Twitter).

———

Let me turn to what I believe is the broader societal benefit of networking. Sharing ideas and information gives us a deeper understanding of ourselves, but it also contributes to making us better at our jobs and better citizens.

Think about all the community clubs in every city and town across the country. Think about what they contribute — the Lions Club, Kinsmen, Kiwanis, Rotary, and others. These organizations provide a platform for networking, but they are also vehicles to come together to create community benefits. The fundraising efforts, the volunteer work, the sense of pride in the collective are all benefits. Chambers of commerce and other business organizations not only create benefits for the members but also contribute to the fabric of the broader community. The collective does create more energy than the sum of the individuals.

The idea that networking benefits not just the individual but the broader society was an important concept behind the creation of the MaRS building at the corner of University Avenue and College Street in Toronto. At the beginning of this century, Dr. John Evans and a group of visionary leaders championed the idea of creating an innovation centre where investors and scientists, businesspeople and academics, would co-locate.

The physical space is purpose-built for creating opportunities to network. Built on the theory of cluster economics and convergence innovation, the idea is that if people are physically co-located, they feed off each other's energy. The interaction between business and the scientific community stimulates innovation and creativity that might otherwise not have happened.

Dr. Evans came to see me when I was in government and made a compelling case for enhancing Ontario's innovation agenda. He wanted to bring Bay Street business investors closer to the medical innovators on University Avenue. Creating opportunities to network across disciplines, he explained, would enhance and stimulate innovation, investment, and economic opportunity. With the support of the government of the day, MaRS, which stands for Medical and Related Sciences, was built to be a networking hub.

So, networking isn't just a benefit for the individual — it creates social and economic benefits for the broader society. Learning how to be a good networker is good for your career and mental well-being, but it is also good for your industry, your community, and for the broader society.

Even if you are an introvert, you can be a good networker. All it takes is a little creativity and a deliberate plan to move outside your comfort zone. You will benefit, those you contact will also benefit, and together you can and will contribute to better social and economic outcomes for your community.

**David Lindsay** is the chair of Infrastructure Ontario's board of directors and the former Ontario deputy minister and principal secretary to the premier of Ontario. He has a wealth of public policy experience and a proven track record in the leadership of public sector organizations, and he has served on more than a dozen boards of directors.

At different times in his career, David has served as president and CEO of the Council of Ontario Universities and president and CEO of Colleges Ontario, the advocacy organization for the province's colleges of applied arts and technology. He also served a term as president and CEO of the Forest Products Association of Canada based in Ottawa.

# THE PEOPLE ON THE BUS

## Shelagh Paul | Head of Global Communications for OMERS

The workday was done, but the real work was just starting as I watched the bus pull up. I took a deep breath, put on a brave smile, and boarded. It felt like I was leaving for summer camp — only my fellow campers were the executive team at the insurance company I worked for early in my career.

It sounded like a great opportunity when I was asked to fill in for my boss at the time, a last-minute switch-up. In a trip that was part team building and part business development, I'd be travelling from Toronto to western Canada for a week with a dozen leaders, meeting employees and insurance brokers in many corners of the country along the way.

I felt so fortunate for the chance to experience Canada's boundless beauty and, of course, to connect with colleagues and business partners on their home turf. But, like many in early career stages, in my twenties I barely knew how to "do corporate" from 9 to 5, let alone be "on" for 168 hours straight.

As the doors closed and the bus began to pull away from the curb, it became very real — there was no backing out now. So, I chose to lean into what would ultimately become a week-long networking boot camp that would change my career trajectory.

The autumn leaves connected the horizon like a quilt as we travelled north to the Sleeping Giant in Thunder Bay. Stood at Terry Fox's monument. Crossed the top of Lake Huron into Winnipeg. Drove through endless golden wheat fields to eventually be greeted by the majestic Canadian Rockies, and finally, arrived in serene coastal Vancouver. It was mesmerizing. The stops in-between, meeting local teams and brokers, were just as memorable. Everyone was excited to host us. And I was just as excited to meet them. I was also intrigued by the opportunity to watch how my executive bus-mates would engage with room after room of strangers. Harnessing my genuine curiosity to learn and listen, I noted their styles were all different. Some were relationship rock stars, working each room, lighting faces up in a heartbeat, drawing people in. Others, quite frankly, weren't. It was in the contrast between styles that I learned my first networking lesson: Building a network is not about you or what you have to offer. It is about being quick to recognize what others need and what you can give — a thought, an ear, a stage, an idea, a smile — in that moment or over the long term.

Our journey home would offer the next real networking lesson — lean in, and when it feels difficult, lean in more. Driving non-stop from Vancouver to Toronto, we dropped down to Spokane, Washington, and then shot straight across the northern U.S., just south of the border. We paused only for meals and fuel. For forty-eight hours, the bus became our world. It was where we slept (thankfully, in sleeping bags on beds), brushed our teeth, and dressed for the day. We spent the time in focused strategy sessions as well as watching movies and playing games — *endless* rounds of Yahtzee. Constantly conversing and sharing stories.

I'll pause to let my experience sink in . . . This is *a lot* of face time with anyone, let alone co-workers and your CEO!

And at the risk of dating myself, there was no technology to dive into for a moment of escape, to regroup. Phones simply rang back then — they were not mini-computers with access to texts, emails, news, videos, music, podcasts, or audiobooks. iPads had not yet been invented. Our time together on that leg of the journey was just that — completely uninterrupted time together. A constant stream of inbound questions from people who were more experienced than me. People who held power and influence. People I wanted to learn from and impress. This trip mattered.

I'll admit, at times I didn't feel "on." I certainly didn't think I was ready to be in their presence full-time, to take up space and use my voice. I mostly focused on ensuring I didn't say the wrong thing, more than I even tried to say the right thing. In hindsight, this focus likely prompted me to actively embrace each interaction. I asked questions and listened to their stories. Eventually I felt comfortable enough to reciprocate and share my own.

All our cross-country moments together provided an invaluable foundation for how I now think about networking.

I don't.

Networking, as we've come to love or hate it, is a transactional exercise. For me, a better frame is simply prioritizing the value of connection in your life and embracing every interaction as an opportunity to create or strengthen a relationship with someone. Connecting with people can become a passion. Sometimes it's easy, natural. Other times, it requires a commitment to showing up curious, authentic, and empathetic every day.

## THE EARLY BIRD GETS THE CAKE

Many of the people I spent time building connections with early in life are now executives, owners, authors, lawyers, board members, teachers, doctors — impressive subject matter experts, and most definitely impressive humans. Yes, I'm extremely proud to know each of them and am in awe of who they've become, but I was equally proud when I added them to my network long before they reached these career heights. Admiration aside, I wanted them in my circle from the get-go because they challenged how I thought about the world. Because I saw their value and how learning from them would cultivate mine.

In 2010, I was in a leadership role with the same Canadian insurer when the Ontario government pushed through significant auto insurance reforms. The demanding timelines and scope required concentrated resources from all corners of the industry to provide uniform education to Ontario consumers on the changes and choices ahead. I found myself seated at a table with industry leaders and peers and the regulator — at the time, it was a table full of strangers.

We met weekly and it was all business. There was barely time for anything else. After several exhausting months of debate and challenge, we successfully reached the finish line. I remember thinking "now what?" as I looked to the chairperson of the working group during our final meeting. What came next was a phrase I have yet to hear expressed again in my professional career: "Let's have cake to celebrate," they said. And we did.

Celebration was in order, we had done good and important work, but there was an opportunity bigger than boardroom cake here.

My life at the time was a delicate balancing act — well, at least it was an act I was attempting to balance. I had two young children: Matthew was almost four, and Liam was just one. I was freshly back to work in a new, demanding executive role with a one-hour train commute each way. I wasn't sure how I'd find the time to socialize after work, but there was something about three members of the working group that really impressed me. Their perspectives were different, smart, and inspiring, and so were they. I wanted to know more about them, their career journeys to this point, what made them tick.

I could let this opportunity slip by, or I could prioritize getting to know them. The day following the "cake meeting," I sent an email expressing my gratitude for having had time with them, ending my message with a simple ask: "Want to meet for 'cake' after work someday?" (And by cake, let's face it, I probably meant a cocktail.) It was a decision that opened the door to a crew I would grow to appreciate well beyond my chapter in that industry.

Prioritize investing in new connections early — when nothing is at stake.

The four of us met four times a year for the next decade — our "caketails" turned into full meals. We'd rotate responsibility for booking dinner at a different Toronto restaurant. We found the time to schedule this outing without fail — until the COVID-19 pandemic hit. We shared many laughs. We were vulnerable, opening up about personal challenges. We prioritized our dinners together. We supported each other through changes and challenges. We celebrated career triumphs. I learned something new every time we were together.

Are we best friends? No, not really. In fact, we don't even share many interests. However, our differences and respect for one another is the magic in our connection. To this day, I can rely on any member of that crew to answer my call, and they can similarly count on me. In fact, I tested it when I was writing this chapter — a quick LinkedIn message to one who has relocated to Vancouver resulted in an immediate response that included plans to meet for dinner on her next visit to Toronto.

## MRS. HAY AND THE ART OF APPRECIATION

Mrs. Hay was my grade school history teacher. A force of nature dressed in bold outfits, she exuded kindness, intellect, and wit. With her legendary booming voice, she held every one of us to a high standard and demanded excellence in everything we set our minds to. She was no-nonsense. The teacher you wouldn't dare pull a fast one on, Mrs. Hay was also someone you never wanted to let down.

Now with two teenagers of my own, I'm in awe of how she bravely led groups of eighty or so thirteen-year-old girls on field trips, every year — something I wouldn't likely dare attempt. We travelled by bus to Ottawa to visit the Royal Canadian Mint and the country's politicians.

To Quebec to walk the Plains of Abraham. And to Washington, where many of the big decisions are made. Cool opportunities to see and experience history, right? It was, but what has stuck with me more than the landmarks and monuments, more than our fun and activities, is the practice she made our highest priority: the art of expressing thanks. On every trip, each student was expected to pre-write thank-you notes to every person who gave their time to us. The parents and bus drivers who tolerated our antics. The politicians who welcomed us into their offices. The tour guides. Grading for thoughtfulness, Mrs. Hay didn't accept a basic thank-you: Each note needed to be researched to ensure a personal touch, be handwritten, and be personally delivered in the moment.

Although thank-you notes are rare these days, the act of expressing appreciation is essential to how I greet each day and central to how I build and maintain my connections.

Practising appreciation is different from practising gratitude. Appreciation is simply about recognizing the moments, people, events, or things that bring you a spark of pure joy. Gratitude is often a more significant acknowledgement of thanks for something that makes your life better. The difference is something I recently learned via a podcast, and now I am compelled to practise both in my life in various ways. These days, I spend a few minutes every morning — on the same one-hour commute — listing ten things I have appreciated in the last twenty-four hours. Logged in my phone, they are things that simply made me smile or stopped me in my tracks. The most difficult part of this practice is that you aren't permitted to repeat anything on your list — ever. If I could, my 110-pound Bernese mountain dog, Wilson, would always dominate the list.

This practice has me digging deep daily to identify new things I appreciate. And slowly it has changed my outlook. I have begun to look for, notice, and value the smallest of details about people, places, experiences, and things. Bright colours. Thanksgiving dinner. A joke from Liam. A kind gesture. The beauty in sunlight. Art, in all forms. A great piece of advice. I've become more present and ensure the people who make my daily list know it — I show my appreciation of them through gratitude, by saying thank you in the moment or the next day. It matters.

Gratitude is a powerful human emotion that builds and sustains long-term relationships. Tell people what you learned from them or why spending time with them mattered to you. Make time to thank people. Prioritize it. Get — *and give* — what Mrs. Hay would consider an A+.

## NETWORKING ISN'T CHILD'S PLAY

The moon is streaming into my son's dark room. "Good night," I whisper, as I head to the door.

"Mom, wait. Come back," he murmurs. My heart stops. He is now a teen. This is rare.

"What's up?"

"Remember the two questions we used to ask each other every night when I was little?"

"Of course I do! One, what was one moment today that made you genuinely happy? And two, what is your one do-over moment of the day, the thing you'd handle differently if you could?"

"Yeah, those . . . why did we do that?"

"Well, there are a few reasons. It was how I learned about your world. It gave you a chance to express yourself, to listen and ask questions. It was a way for me to feel and do the same. And mostly, it was just a really nice way to end the day."

"We should start it again."

"Definitely, let's."

These moments remind me of why I prioritize connection. With my children, colleagues, friends — everyone. And they remind me of why it's important to drop everything on my mind — adulting, work priorities, *whatever* — to be present, and often simply to listen, and not always when it suits me. And to teach others to do the same.

Being conscious of how I show up for myself and others every day — open, curious, authentic, empathetic — is what networking is supposed to be. This isn't child's play. Sometimes it requires a deep breath, investment, even hard work.

The art in networking lies in our ability to spot and engage in these moments. To really connect with someone regardless of age, stage, influence. I try to actively participate in every opportunity I find myself in. It's always worth the effort — especially in the long term.

## CHOOSE BRIDGES OVER BOTS

Being asked to contribute my perspective to this collection of networking insights is an honour — and a slightly daunting one at that. I wanted to use all the knowledge I could access, so for this final vignette I checked in with artificial intelligence (AI), our modern-day communicator, to challenge myself: Was there a new way to think about networking that perhaps I was overlooking?

I grabbed my phone. "Can AI tools help with person-to-person networking?" I typed into ChatGPT.

I breathed a sigh of relief as the bot validated my perspective: "Networking is being thoughtful and intentional with the connections you grow with other people." It then offered very smart ways to get organized for the task. Research we might do. Platforms we can use. Overall, a decent place to start.

But, once we are organized, AI won't help us make or maintain real human connection. There are no replacements and no shortcuts.

My network is my trusted community. It ranges from friends to current and former colleagues I've shared experiences with — people I see often and others I wish I could engage with more. People younger and older with vastly different experiences and interests. Wonderful, smart humans I would gladly help in any way, knowing they are ready to reciprocate.

Some relationships were forged quickly and others over decades, but in each case, we built a bridge that will lead either one of us, at any given time, to future-facing conversations and opportunities — and also back to a safe place for reflection, learning, support, and validation.

So, here's my bottom line: There are no hacks, tips, or secrets that will elevate your networking game for the long term. Make building your community a way of life. Prioritize connection, be present and intentional in every moment possible. Lean in. Listen and learn. Care deeply and say thank you. Spend more time with humans building bridges than with bots.

**Shelagh Paul** is OMERS' senior vice-president and head of global communications, helping deliver a sustainable, affordable, and meaningful Defined Benefit Pension Plan for 600,000-plus members. The hallmark of her career success lies in her ability to spark and nurture powerful relationships. She is sought after for her thoughtful counsel and recognized for her ability to cultivate environments where everyone can deliver their best work.

Prior to OMERS, Shelagh worked at the Dominion of Canada General Insurance Company and Travelers Canada, where she helped to expand broker-based insurance marketing in Canada.

# CURIOUS, GRATEFUL, AND PEOPLE-FIRST: NETWORKING FOR FUTURE LEADERS

### Baron Manett | Founder of Per Se Brand Experience

In today's ever-connected world, there is much discussion around technology, apps, AI, and what's next. All these tools promise to help supercharge our work and careers. But I believe that the people in my network have helped to activate my career exponentially more than any technology or work tool I have tried. The power of relationships and professional networking is essential for people aiming to develop long-term career success.

If you look across our digital social networks, it can often be overwhelming. A quick look at the professional social network LinkedIn, with over 950 million members across 200 countries, makes it seem on the surface that everyone is connecting at scale. However, authentic networking, which is the process of making and building sustainable and value-added professional relationships, is a human experience. One could say that networking is one of the original social networks. In a world where competition for professional opportunities is fiercer than ever, building a solid personal brand and forging meaningful connections is a vital skill for career success. That age-old saying is only half true: "It's not what you know, but who you know" now should read, "It's what you know *and* who you know." Personal connections matter. Networking is no longer just a buzzword; it's a critical skill that will drive your career momentum to new heights.

The importance of developing and maintaining key business relationships is a skill that can be learned and practised over time. Networking is about more than just collecting names and attending events. It's not about having the most connections or knowing the most people. Professional network development is a long-term, strategic practice best enabled through gratitude, a future-forward mindset, and a genuine focus on curiosity and mutual service — a natural feeling of connection with and caring for the people around you. The desire to help people succeed will help your networking efforts go far and deliver career fulfillment and success. Successful networking and professional connections are based on gratitude and generosity.

## THE POWER OF GRATEFUL NETWORKING

Connecting with colleagues is a two-way street. When I began my professional career, I was a young business graduate. I was intimidated to reach out to people I did not know, or many "leaders" directly, or colleagues who were more senior or more accomplished. Anyone you may look up to and want to meet has also been there. "Why would they want to meet with me?" "They won't return my call or email." "People are too busy." There are many excuses, and sometimes the person may decline. However, over my career, I can count the people who said no to meeting with me on one hand. I have been blessed to have had a series of good mentors; one is my father-in-law, Norman Paul.

Norman has a fantastic network of people due to his many successes in business and philanthropy. He would always say to me, "You won't score any goals on the bench. Get out on the ice, skate around, and see what happens." Whenever I was shy about reaching out to a new contact (and at times today, I still get that way), I think of this comment, and he's right: We must let ourselves be seen. Networking is an active exercise and needs to be supported throughout your career. Most people are open to meeting passionate people whom they may work or collaborate with in the future. Don't forget that when you think of reaching out to colleagues to meet, discuss a matter, or request help with one, each person does have the option to say no. However, when your colleague says yes to a call or meeting, that person gives you a gift — their time, experience, and point of view. Be grateful for this gift and opportunity.

I was fortunate to meet David Tsubouchi in 2004 due to active networking. I had never met David up to that time, and we worked in different professions. But I was working on a project, and a colleague mentioned Mr. Tsubouchi as an expert in the area I was working on. I wanted to connect with David, but his impressive career and credentials made me doubt that he would have the time or interest in talking to me. I ignored those doubts, got up my courage, and called David. To my surprise, not only did he make time for me, but he invited me to lunch. He appreciated that I reached out and was interested in my work. We have since worked together on several projects, and I'm very proud and grateful to call him a colleague and friend for the past twenty years.

Networking always starts with a first step. When the people you want to meet with say yes, that is a great feeling. You can show gratitude in fundamental, vital ways, and being prepared for your time with a person is one of the best ways to do this. Do your research, learn, and prepare to maximize the opportunity. This will show your invited colleague you respect their time, expertise, and openness to meeting with you. Leading each outreach with the idea of gratitude is the foundation upon which successful networking is built. Author and marketing leader Jay Baer aptly says, "When it comes to growing strong connections, a simple 'thank you' can go a long way." Expressing genuine appreciation for others' time, insights, and contributions fosters a rapport of trust and respect. Saying thank you is always in

---

\*    Jay Baer, "Youtility Real Estate," *Youtility: Why Smart Marketing Is About Help Not Hype* (Portfolio, 2013).

style. The old-fashioned, handwritten thank-you note is still one of the best personal brand tools you can utilize (and I use it to this day). Saying thank you is a fantastic way to stand out and be remembered. Leading with gratitude will help you establish meaningful connections and ultimately will help pave the way for collaborative partnerships.

My career as a marketing professional, producer, and professor, along with my personal focus areas as a husband, father, and friend, have been exponentially improved through the idea of networking and purposeful outreach. I have met so many wonderful people who have helped me and that I've had the honour of helping. While gratitude is the cornerstone of networking, I have observed some key mindsets that the best professional networkers continuously practise for success. These individuals would not be where they are without their colleagues' and network's kindness and help with development. Successful networkers are optimistic, have a mindset for the future, and are consistently curious and passionate about developing a mutual value exchange with the people they meet and connect with. Keeping these ideas in mind will help guide your career outreach and improve the quality and reach of your networks.

## SUCCESSFUL CONNECTORS ARE OPTIMISTS

The actions and care you take in building your professional bench of colleagues and relationships are part of a process that takes time and effort. Networking is not about the present moment; it is an investment in your future. As former first lady Michelle Obama observes, "It's about the difference you make in people's lives."* The best connectors I have met are optimists at heart. They believe tomorrow will be better than today and bring more ideas and opportunities than others. This mindset enables curiosity and long-term thinking. Connecting professionally is not a quid pro quo exercise. It's born from a mutual

---

\* Michelle Obama, Democratic National Convention, September 4, 2012.

respect and an interest in connecting with people you admire and may work with in the future. Some of the relationships I value most are people I haven't worked with directly yet, but I hope I will, and I want them to succeed.

Connecting with various individuals also gives you access to a wealth of knowledge and insights that can shape your personal and professional growth. Focus on 360-degree connections — colleagues who are at all levels of their careers and influence. A variety of talents and perspectives only makes your network stronger. Adopting a forward-looking mindset means seeking connections that align with your goals and aspirations, helping you stay ahead of industry trends, and ultimately positioning yourself as a respected and sought-after colleague in your field of choice.

## SHARED INTERESTS AND VALUES

Successful networking cannot be a self-serving activity; human relationships thrive on reciprocity and mutual benefit. Who you reach out to and focus on should never be solely about selling or personal gain but rather a genuine desire to help others. Building relationships based on a foundation of shared values and interests is crucial. By identifying ways to add value to others' lives or careers without expecting an immediate return, you cultivate a network of trust and goodwill that will be reciprocated in the long run.

Gone are the days of aggressive sales pitches and pushing your agenda at networking events. People want to help and be helped. Taking the time to listen, understand others' needs, and offer your assistance are beautiful ways to stand out. By genuinely investing in others' success and striving to be a valuable resource, you position yourself as a trusted adviser and a go-to person within your network. This service-first approach creates more robust connections and opens doors to new business opportunities. Networking is a two-way street. It's never about what you can get from others but how we can add value to our colleagues' goals. True networking is a value exchange. Each professional relationship you develop can be built on mutual benefit.

## NETWORK EFFECTS

Maintaining professional relationships requires consistent effort. To this day, I work to meet new colleagues each week and actively keep in touch with my network. Regularly check in with your connections, share updates on your endeavours, and offer assistance whenever possible. The key to effective networking is to keep it top of mind and remain active.

I recently met a new colleague, Andrea Torraville of Sobeys, in Calgary. She is a wonderfully energetic and empathetic talent leader. Her comment sums it up very well: "We meet amazing people, we connect, and it's a fantastic start. But there's more to the story, and that's where the real magic happens — maintaining those relationships. . . . Some connections will stay with you forever, others will come and go, and that's perfectly okay. Gain contacts, lose contacts — it's all part of the journey. The key is to be genuine, approach every interaction with good intentions, and focus on the learning and value it adds to your life."[*]

A periodic email, a call, or even a social media interaction can help maintain a thriving community of which you're the active leader. It's your network and you can set the goals. As business author Sahil Bloom observes, "Surround yourself with people thinking big about the future, [and] you'll build a beautiful one."[**]

---

[*]  Andrea Torraville, "Building & Maintaining Networks," LinkedIn, 2023, https://www .linkedin.com/posts/andreatorraville_how-to-a-build-and-maintain-relationship-activity -7117870689197428737-Qi5_?utm_source=share&utm_medium=member_desktop.

[**]  Sahil Bloom (@SahilBloom), X (formerly Twitter), May 12, 2023, 8:19 a.m., https://x.com /SahilBloom/status/1656997541303468033. The full post is: "Important realization: Your environment sets your reality. Surround yourself with people who are constantly talking about the past, you'll be stuck in it. Surround yourself with people who are thinking big about the future, you'll build a beautiful one. Find your tribe."

## WE ARE KNOWN BY THE COMPANY WE KEEP

Networking is a skill that is most powerful and impactful when practised diligently and approached with openness and gratitude. By adopting a future-forward mindset, focusing on mutual interest and service, and shifting our perspective from selling to helping, we can unlock the true potential of networking for career success. Networking holds even greater significance today, when we are so often online or behind our screen. In the words of New York University professor Scott Galloway, "Talk to people. Risk awkwardness, embarrassment, and rejection. Mingle with people your age, older people, younger people."*

The value placed on true relationships continues to grow. So, step out of your comfort zone, take a step off the bench, and go for a skate on the ice. Embrace the power of networking and watch as your career reaches new heights through the meaningful connections you create. In an increasingly interconnected world, your professional network is your most valuable asset. Embrace it, nurture it, invest in it, and let it guide you towards your professional aspirations.

---

\* Scott Galloway, *The Algebra of Happiness: Notes on the Pursuit of Success, Love, and Meaning* (Portfolio, 2019).

**Baron Manett** founded Per Se Brand Experience, a brand experience consultancy focused on helping organizations reach, relate, and grow successfully and sustainably. As one of Canada's leading brand builders and a frequent speaker on brand experience, content marketing, and audience engagement, his work has been recognized with business growth and national and international industry recognition. Baron's work has also contributed to the marketing success of many leading brand organizations, including RBC, Visa, Conagra Brands, Unilever, the Student's Commission of Canada, Ontario's Ministry of Tourism, and TD Bank.

# BE A GIVER, NOT A TAKER

### David Tsubouchi | Former Solicitor General and Chair of Treasury/Management Board of Ontario

When I talk to young people, they ask me how they can make their way in the world. Believe me when I say I understand their struggles. My experience as a boy was no different than every other Japanese Canadian family. So many new immigrants' stories begin with coming to Canada with twenty dollars in their pocket and working hard to succeed.

My family did that just like everyone else. Both of my grandmothers cleaned houses for rich people in Vancouver. One of my grandfathers was a gardener for those same people and the other one worked as a lumberjack. They worked hard and bought houses. Then the government stole everything from us: houses, businesses, money, and personal possessions.

When they were released from the prison camps, they had to start again with nothing. When I was growing up, we had very little. We didn't go to movies. We had no books in our house, as they were considered a luxury. But I never considered myself as being disadvantaged because I had a good family.

Canada was a very different place then from how it is now. There were very few people of visible minorities. I was the only one in my public school. In the 1950s, people hated anyone of Japanese descent and the bigotry was much more overt than it is today. When you add the fact that we had very little, and that I was the smallest and youngest kid in my grade because I was accelerated through school, it's no wonder I was a social outcast. I was more concerned with being accepted than with networking.

By the time I was ten years old, I had read every biography in the school library because I wanted to know what these successful people did when they were young to accomplish what they eventually did. I had two takeaways. First they had perseverance, as they all had failures on the road to success. And second, they never did it all on their own.

When I went to high school, I was a shrimp. I was barely over five feet tall and not quite a hundred pounds. Getting good marks was not a problem, and I was a pretty good athlete for my size. I was too small for football, so I did cross-country running. I loved music, so I joined the band and learned how to play the clarinet. Magically, between Grades 9 and 10, I got my growth spurt, and then I played football. I played and excelled in most sports, including gymnastics (pommel horse), wrestling, track, hockey, and badminton. It was then that the penny dropped.

Sports had elevated me to some degree of social acceptance, so I was in with the jock group. I eventually became the president of the band and played first clarinet, so I was in with the band geeks. I also got top marks, so I was in with the brains. I was probably the only one who was able to connect with all three of these social groups in high school. Suddenly, I understood what networking was.

My other big breakthrough in high school was with my self-image. Originally, I was shy and lacked confidence. For years I had been called racial slurs like "dirty Jap" or "Chink." I had been bullied in grade school and beaten up.

Being a social outcast was worse. Never being invited when other kids were. Although I told myself that I was going to be better than all of them, I became very introverted. I couldn't speak to more than two people without looking at my shoes and muttering. Even though my parents told me to be proud of who I was, the rest of the world was telling me differently.

Many years later, when I met George Takei, who we all know as Sulu on *Star Trek*, I told him that he changed my life. I told him that before he came along, all East Asians had been portrayed as bad, evil characters in movies and television, or as ridiculous caricatures like Mickey Rooney in *Breakfast at Tiffany's* with buck teeth and a bad accent. Then he came along and was an action hero. Suddenly, I thought that maybe it was cool to look like me.

## THE SECRET OF SUCCESS: BE LIKE SAINT TEDDY

There are many so-called truisms for getting ahead in business, like "nice guys finish last" and "never give a sucker an even break." This is a formula for crash-and-burn failure. People who try to take advantage of others quickly gain a reputation for doing so, and bad news travels fast.

Treating others fairly and with integrity breeds opportunity. Would you rather deal with someone who says "we should do this because we can get away with it" or someone you can trust? Not a difficult question to answer.

Years ago, I was asked to be "partners" in a business venture. Partners to me means 50/50, unless it is specified differently. The venture was successful, but in year one it was 70/30 — and not in my favour. Year two was 90/10 and year three was 100/0. This result was more or less my fault due to my assuming that others could be just as trustworthy. I chalked this up to experience and went on with my life.

A few years later I was approached by the same person with respect to another transaction I was working on as he wanted to be a part of it. When I told him I could not work with him, I had to explain to him that it was because he had no integrity. His reaction was that he could write me a cheque. That was definitely not the point.

On the positive side, there is my friend Ted Manziaris. Ted is the nicest, kindest person I know. He is packed with integrity. Not only would I give

Ted the shirt off my back, but I only wish I could be as good a person as he is. Ted's secret to success is to treat everyone fairly and kindly.

Years ago, I was waiting for someone to show up for a lunch appointment at Il Fornello, a restaurant in Etobicoke, when a young fellow walked up to my table and handed his cell phone to me. "I have someone on my phone who wants to talk to you," he said.

"Hello?" I said.

"Dave, it's Aris," said Aris Kaplanis. "This phone belongs to Ted Manziaris. He saw you come in and wanted to meet you."

That is how I met Ted. He is one of the most generous people I know. When Ted walks into any room, he lights it up. He owned a company, Turtle Island Recycling, that he had started after he graduated from university. When he began, his entire resources consisted of himself and his mother's K-car.

Ted is a great marketer and handed his card to everyone. He received a call one day from Maple Leaf Gardens. The Gardens was holding a concert on the weekend and wanted to give him an opportunity, so they asked Ted if he could do it, not realizing of course that it was just Ted and his mother's car.

Ted worked all night and day and made an unbelievable number of trips to the dump to get the job done. Maple Leaf Gardens was so pleased that they offered Ted the opportunity to bid for a contract they had with another company when it expired. From that willingness to work, Ted parlayed Turtle Island into a multi-million-dollar business.

Of course Ted works hard but it's his positive attitude, fairness, and kindness that gets him in the door and earns repeat business and referrals. It doesn't hurt that he is sincere in his intentions. Ted has since sold his business and is a volunteer and philanthropist.

There is another sign of success that hangs around Ted's neck. All his friends are happy for him and his success. Nobody thinks of how they can take advantage of Ted or is envious of his achievements. There it is, stated very simply: Live your life with integrity and good intent, and success will follow.

## OPPORTUNITY CALLING

My old friend Danny Leung was over at our house for Thanksgiving dinner, and we were talking about our adventures over the years. As it is in life and in business, we've both had successes and setbacks. Life does not follow your intended and carefully planned path. You do need to set a direction, and you really need perseverance. What is essential is to have a strong belief in yourself. It is great to have friends and colleagues to encourage you and commiserate when you are down, but over time many will come and go. It is your life and under your control.

When I was young, I did not have a family that was connected. We were far from that. My father was a dry-cleaning presser who worked hard enough that one day he bought the store that he had toiled at for years. My mother mended clothes for the store and ran the front counter.

My father once said to me that I should never turn down an opportunity because you never know when the next one will show up. By and large, he was right. Using 100 percent hindsight, there were a few I should have said no to. But what he was saying was that sometimes we need to learn on the job.

I am not complaining. I had two advantages in life that many people don't have. I had a great family — we struggled, but we struggled together. I also got an education.

The point is that opportunities were few and far between.

My friend Danny's life was like that as well. He came to Canada from Hong Kong and spoke very little English. He got a job as a door-to-door vacuum salesman and sold a vacuum on his first day with basically no English.

Later, he got a job as a commissioned salesman in the men's department at Simpson's in Toronto. At that time, I had just graduated as a young lawyer and Danny was making three times what I made. He once sold a hundred suits in a day.

He then graduated to the gaming industry and eventually became the vice-president of marketing at a major U.S. casino. He has since been involved in many international business ventures. Danny's success has been due to his understanding of what his customers need and treating them with respect.

Danny and I share the view that every phone call, every meeting, and every email may be an opportunity. Of course, the more successful you become, the more this is true, but we have never lost the mentality of what it is like to be poor.

When someone calls me on the weekend or late at night, I am always happy to get the call. It is evident in my voice. People are more willing to work with someone who appreciates the opportunity, and there's nothing wrong with being positive. But opportunities are only helpful if you recognize them and then act on them.

Of course, as I have already stated, not everything works out the way you thought, but if you're not open to opportunities, you will not hear them knock.

## LINKEDIN

I never thought about having a presence on social media until my friend Colleen Fleming, who at the time was the chair of the Board of Governors of Seneca College (and I was a board member), asked me if I was on LinkedIn. This was back in 2013. I told her I wasn't, and she explained the advantages of it. I decided on her advice to give it a go. That was one of my better decisions.

LinkedIn is the first place I look to check up on someone who wants to do business or connect with me. It is also the first place I look when someone applies for a position. That is followed up by looking at other social media. The beautiful thing about LinkedIn is that you write your own story. Take your time and look at other profiles that strike you as engaging. (Mine is probably not a good example because I just list things that I have done, and I am not actively seeking anything.)

Be a Giver, Not a Taker | 63

Over the years, I have received many invitations through LinkedIn to join corporate boards, most of which I have not accepted, but some I do. There is a certain amount of due diligence in joining a board of directors that is accompanied by monetary and fiduciary duties, not to mention liabilities.

I have received many requests for meetings and phone calls. The one thing that we are all limited in is time, so that means making choices. Many of us get sucked into taking things on that are not in our best interests or the best use of our time. Occasionally, I have to take inventory of my time and say no to people. Firstly, I am not an employment agency, so don't ask me for a job. Secondly, if your reason for talking to me is purely in your own self-interest, don't bother. But occasionally, someone gets my interest and we have a connection. Sometimes it results in some mentoring, or some advice garnered from experience, and sometimes I find a kindred spirit and friend. Relationships are two-way streets, which is not to say they are quid pro quo because that would be bargaining for something that's the least I could do. Generosity of spirit is the key. On one hand I am saying be careful with your time, and on the other, be generous with like-minded people.

Someone asked me lately how I was able to attract over 35,000 followers on LinkedIn. Here are a few suggestions:

1. I post regularly. My area is leadership. Occasionally, one of my posts goes viral (I had one that was viewed over 1.6 million times).

2. When someone congratulates me on an anniversary or new position, I thank them.

3. I am happy when one of my connections gets a new job or earns an award or academic credential. These are times to be proud of and I congratulate them.

4. I am *not* an open networker and reserve the right to reject fake profiles (and I do look at backgrounds). I will accept any reasonable request.

5. If I see a disrespectful comment that someone has made on a post, I delete it and will block the person. My page is a place where I expect respectful dialogue.

What astonishes me when I see profiles on LinkedIn is the number of people who either have no photo or have one in which they look sour or dour. You only have one chance to make a first impression, and the first thing people see is your photo.

Of course, if you have no photo, you are somewhat anonymous. Many people cannot be bothered looking at your background. It raises other questions as to the legitimacy of your profile or your professionalism. Why isn't there a photo?

Most executives I know check social media about candidates for positions. It is highly informative. I assume that anyone who gets that far in the process has the academic and professional credentials. What usually interests me besides work is what defines this person. Do they volunteer? Do they have any other interests? One candidate had competed in triathlons. That told me that this person had dedication and commitment.

But the first place I look is the photo. It doesn't have to be professional quality, but it cannot be cheesy. Look like you want the position, the work, or the relationship. Wear professional clothes. Do not put your photo upside down or in some strange position to attract attention. You may attract attention, but will you get the job?

Think of your background. Do not take the photo in a bathroom or bedroom. Make sure that nothing in the background looks strange, like horns from your head or a funny sign — unless, of course, your objective is to be a joker. But save that for Facebook.

Lastly and most importantly: smile. Everyone wants to work with a positive person. My colleague Annabelle Erne once told me to "hire for attitude and train for skills." I want to work with people who are aspirational and optimistic because they can achieve anything. So, smile in your photo and in your life. It doesn't cost you a penny.

# POLITICS

Politics can bring together people from all different walks of life who have little else in common. Participating in politics is an effective way to reach beyond your comfort zone and develop your networking.

Some simple suggestions: Pick a party that you share some beliefs with and not simply because they are in power. And look for opportunities to volunteer — there will be many because all parties need volunteers — but do so genuinely, not as someone who just wants to rub shoulders.

This is an excellent way to meet people. When you volunteer, you are viewed in a positive way. You become a compatriot in a cause. You are a co-worker. You become a friend. You will meet all kinds of people who you would never get a chance to meet otherwise. Some will be important in politics and business — people way above your pay grade, but who value you as an associate.

I learned this years ago when I was a young lawyer fresh out of law school. I was asked to join the board of directors of the Japanese Canadian Cultural Centre. I was then tasked with exploring the possibility of having the province of Ontario give the JCCC an exemption from property taxes. The province had given other cultural centres a similar exemption.

This could only be done through a private member's bill. Our MPP was Dennis Timbrell, who was a cabinet minister and could not introduce a private member's bill. Dennis suggested that I meet with Don Cousens, who was the MPP for Markham, where I lived. I met with Don and he agreed to sponsor the bill.

The next step was to get the municipality to agree to the bill. At that time, it was the City of North York, where Mel Lastman was the mayor and Marie Labatte was a councillor. I was able to meet with Mel and Marie separately, and they both agreed to support the bill.

The bill was drafted, and Don introduced it and was able to get it passed. Through this process, a young lawyer who was barely wet behind the ears was able to meet not only Mel Lastman and Marie Labatte, but Dennis Timbrell, Don Cousens, and several members of the legislature.

Soon after, Don asked me if I was interested in joining the executive of his riding association. Although I had been apolitical until then, I was curious and agreed. Through the riding association, I was able to meet a who's who of Markham politics and business. When I eventually opened my law firm in Markham, it gave me a number of contacts. Don also asked me to head up the fundraising for the riding, and I was able to meet most of the business leaders of Markham. It was a lot of work but led to many contacts whom I would ordinarily never have met.

This is something anyone can do. I was a nobody and didn't know anybody. I was the first one in my family to go to university. I had no clue when I went to law school what the life of a lawyer was like. I struggled to get an articling job. When I graduated, there were very few visible minorities in law. Law firms that offered me positions after I was a cabinet minister wouldn't even give me an interview when I graduated. I had no clients. I had no money. I only had hope, determination, and perseverance. If I could do it, anyone can.

A few other lessons from politics can be applied to business and opportunities. Admittedly, politics are more polarized and mean-spirited today, but if you look at the people who have navigated their post-politics lives successfully, they were viewed as the reasonable ones who stuck to the issues and did not indulge in personal attacks. Many of those are my friends who have done well. Janet Ecker, Dan Newman, and Chris Hodgson come to mind.

This is even more important these days with social media. Remember that everyone carries a camera on their phones. Once you say it, it is permanent, widely broadcast, and repeated. Think about what you post or say publicly. If you indulge in personal attacks, it is a race to the bottom.

One more suggestion is to attend events like golf tournaments and fundraising dinners. They are both excellent ways of meeting people. In my two terms as an MPP, I have never sat in my seat at the table past the soup course. I would go table to table and meet people. At the end of the night, my pocket would be stuffed with business cards. You may not be a cabinet minister, but people at these events love to talk politics and meet others. Get off your seat and circulate. The point is not to eat the dinner, regardless of how expensive it is, but to take the opportunity to network.

After the event and you have collected a few business cards, do the old-school thing of sending a note that it was nice meeting the person. If the person is in politics, offering your assistance is never a bad idea.

When I was a cabinet minister, I used to get over twenty requests to meet a day. At most, I had the time for one meeting a day. My staff would go through the requests and present me with a few that would be relevant. The meeting I took would be with someone that either I or my staff had met. Some chance meetings have led to lifelong friendships. But seek possibilities!

## HOW TO ASK

I remember my early teenage years and the stress I went through drumming up the courage to ask a girl out on a date. We had a phone on the wall in the kitchen. Luckily, it had a long cord that I could stretch out into the hall. The first task was to find a time when my parents were not around. This was the simple step.

The more complicated step was what I should say if a) her father answered the phone, b) her mother answered the phone, or c) she answered the phone. If her father answered, I debated if I should just hang up, as there was no caller identification in the old days. I decided to simply ask if my potential date was home. Then the big one: What would I say to her? These overthought steps led to several partial spins on the old rotary phone. Until finally I connected, and I asked.

Was I successful, you might ask? My answer is that a gentleman never tells. What surprises me is that less thought goes into asking someone to meet these days than when I was fourteen years old.

It does matter how you ask. If you approach someone and you sound like a phishing expedition or a scam, it should not surprise you that you will be treated accordingly. Unfortunately, some people actually think it will work and are serious. When someone wants to meet or chat and writes that they have something interesting to tell me or a business proposal that will interest me, it's not difficult to dismiss them. If you have something to say, say it!

At the other extreme are those who have no difficulty just spitting it out that they need my help getting a job. As I mentioned earlier, I am not an employment agency. Especially if I do not know you. I have helped people before and mentored many, but not if you are a stranger.

But there are *ways* of asking. I do like people who show initiative and clarity. Several years ago, I was contacted through LinkedIn by someone who wanted to meet about their business and was looking for some advice. He told me a little about the business and piqued my curiosity. As it was, I had to be in Toronto for several days and was staying in a hotel. I agreed to meet with him for half an hour. He was engaging and knowledgeable, and we ended up talking for three hours. He asked me to be on the advisory committee for his company and I agreed. Since then, Murray Simser and I have become close friends and there is rarely a week that goes by without a long conversation on a variety of topics.

Another close friend, Baron Manett, called me out of the blue because he had an issue that he thought I could help him resolve. He made a cold call to me as I did not know him at all. He got my interest, and I was convinced by his sincerity and the tone of his voice and language. We worked together and the project succeeded.

The hard sell never works. It doesn't matter to me how much money I could make but it *does* matter who I work with. I have learned more from hard lessons than from successes.

Be yourself and be sincere. Give enough information for someone to consider that you are sincere and not some flimflam man. It doesn't always work, but the other way *never* does.

It was a long journey for me to get the courage to speak up and have some self-confidence. But you must have faith in yourself — believe!

**David Tsubouchi** is an author and former politician, regulator, and integrity commissioner. He has served as the MPP for Markham for two terms and held cabinet posts in the Ontario Legislature, including Minister of Consumer and Commercial Relations, Solicitor General, Chair of Management Board/Treasury Board, and Minister of Culture. Prior to being the first Japanese Canadian to be elected to a provincial legislature and appointed to cabinet, David served as a councillor for the Town of Markham for two terms. He currently sits on the board of directors for OMERS Administration Corporation and Tarion.

Having been an international keynote speaker from North America to Asia, he currently lectures on diversity at York University's Department of Equity Studies and politics and governance at the Directors College (McMaster University). His memoir, *Gambatte*, was nominated for the Speaker's Book Award and the Heritage Toronto Award.

# AN ODD COUPLE AND THE VALUE OF NETWORKING

**Marc Kealey | Chief Advocate and Founder of K&A Inc.**

When considering how I could or should contribute to a book about networking, my thinking was that I would offer my own personal perspective on the business and personal value of networking and why it's so much more than building a business or finding a job. This, I believe, qualifies me to offer that perspective. My own experience is that someone may have the skills and education, but without strong personal connections, it can be very difficult for an individual to grow in life and in their career.

Further, many people seem to have trouble with networking largely because they may be introverted or worry that they are asking too much of the people they target, or maybe they just haven't developed their network appropriately. I believe this book could be a simple guide to overcoming those challenges.

———

For me, my personal network in/for business has been honed from practical involvement in politics — and my journey and involvement in politics has spanned over forty years. For this book, I contemplated how a boy from Niagara Falls, Ontario, could aspire to be a co-editor of a book — especially on networking.

Then it dawned on me. As a young boy of fourteen, I became involved in politics compliments of my grandmother and my great-aunt, who were intimately involved in federal politics for years. They instilled in me the confidence for outreach and networking. Both were strong women with massive networks in politics and from their chosen professions — one was a healthcare professional, the other a well-known lawyer and judge. Both were from Ottawa, the cradle of politics in Canada, and both had tremendous confidence and a deep affinity for politics. They believed that how we live is all about politics.

My great-aunt Yvonne was appointed to the bench by John N. Turner, who at the time was the federal minister of justice and later became prime minister. She was always involved in politics and used her network in politics to develop a successful career as a judge. She introduced me to John Turner well before he became leader of the Liberal Party of Canada. (My first job ever was working for Mr. Turner after I left undergraduate school.) My great-aunt stayed close to her network, even when she was obliged to stay out of politics as a judge. Her advice was always pithy: "Politics is how you get a job and is as much about who you know as it is about what you know. Politics is whether you can use cannabis legally, marry someone of the same gender, or drive faster or slower on the freeway. Politics is how much tuition costs, how long unemployment payments last, and how old you have to be to legally have a beer." So, the use of a network — especially in or from politics — can be beneficial.

Being involved in politics afforded me the opportunity to meet exceptional people, and that was a benefit to me personally and professionally. Politics shaped the choice of education I wanted and achieved. Niagara Falls seemed the quintessential hotbed for politics with its consequential Canadians like George Bukator, Judy LaMarsh, Vince Kerrio, Joe Greene, Rob Nicholson, and others who gave me the opportunity to build my own organizational skills in campaigns, develop public policy, and attend events. It was like a free college and gave me the opportunity to build a network that, to this day, is envied and beneficial to me and my community.

My educational and networking choices because of politics afforded me the opportunity to meet people like John Turner — we first met in 1977 — and we stayed close ever since. Because we were connected, I was hired by party officials in 1984 to work on his campaign for the leadership of the Liberal Party and later in his Prime Minister's Office straight out of undergrad. It was my great-aunt, Yvonne, who not only connected us but whose recommendation to Mr. Turner and the team close to him got me the job. My legacy network in politics, which I continued to develop over years of being in practical politics, helped me succeed in my role on Parliament Hill for the half dozen years I worked there.

Even more beneficial is my personal relationship with the co-editor of this book — David Tsubouchi. In short, David exemplifies networking to the max. I believe there is no one better at using his network, benefiting from it, and giving back with it. As background, I knew of David even before we met. When I first heard about him he was a municipal politician and, because I was working for John Turner in Ottawa at the time, it was my responsibility to liaise with provincial and municipal governments. So as a municipal councillor, David was on my radar.

I left politics in 1990 and, following my graduate degree, began a career in hospital administration. I like to think I succeeded in this role because of my skill *and* my network — particularly in politics. I had to keep close relations with elected officials and use my network to benefit the hospital and the community where I worked. In 1995, the government of Ontario changed in a pivotal election. The Conservative Party was elected to a monumental majority, and I learned that David Tsubouchi was elected in a riding northeast of Toronto and was immediately appointed to Premier Mike Harris's cabinet.

Over the coming years, David and I had cause to meet periodically, either at Queen's Park or at political events. My close friendship with him began after a chance phone call he made to me in early 2003. At the time, I was general manager of Atomic Energy of Canada (AECL), having been appointed in 1999 after ten years in the hospital sector. The role — a global one — required a substantial understanding of government, and the benefit of my network from years in politics served me well.

Evidently, David was aware that I had the role and had updated his Rolodex. The reason for his call was vintage networking — he knew AECL needed good communicators, and one of his former staffers was good at communications. He saw a fit and he was on target! He created a benefit for his colleague through an outreach to me. His recommendation and our personal relationship netted his former staffer the role. It was beneficial to both of us — the person David recommended excelled in the role and in fact translated it into a position at the United Nations in subsequent years.

I believe David is one of the best networkers I have ever encountered. While at Queen's Park, MPPs on both sides of the legislature and even his cabinet colleagues often commented on how superb he was at keeping in touch — a card to say thank you, a quick call to check in, or a casual exchange in a hallway just to say hello. Many agreed that David transcends partisan politics and, because he is such a likeable person, it's easy to work with him and stay connected.

In fact, years after I left AECL, David and I remained in contact and, although we had few occasions to see each other, we connected through our networks. In the latter part of the 2000s, I had started my own consulting company and was visiting the Ontario legislature for a meeting with a government official. I saw David sitting in the lobby. Of course, we connected and in vintage Tsubouchi style he made the overture to meet up again, which we did. It was *that* encounter that led to international business opportunities that have been ongoing for the past fifteen years.

———

The lesson in the story of my relationship with David Tsubouchi is that you don't always have to gain something concrete in a networking relationship. As I aspire to offer in this chapter, if you can introduce people who can benefit from one another, it can be effective and meaningful — and that has been my experience in my relationship with David. Over the years we have managed to develop businesses, build upon our networks, and use our mutual connections for professional and personal benefit. This is all despite the fact that, as many know, we are political yin and yang — David is a Conservative and I'm a Liberal. We are a veritable odd couple.

You can build a stronger rapport with multiple people, and you never know where it might lead. There are some key lessons to using a network and making it valuable, and the following are some of mine.

## USE YOUR NETWORK TO CONNECT *AND* RECONNECT

David's lesson is clear: Many of us have networks and contacts, we may even have spent years meeting people, but do we actually develop our connections? And when we do, do we use the contacts effectively? The value of a network is that it's made up of two-way, mutually beneficial relationships, which are the gold standard in business. There must always be mutual benefit, be it personal or professional. Any exchange where there is clear selfish intent is off-putting. When that happens, you may not want to go out of your way for that kind of contact because they haven't put any effort into sustaining the relationship.

After you choose the right people to network with, remember to stay in contact with them. In a world where there is less and less personal touch — when everything is done via email or text — people often appreciate a personal follow-up like a phone call or even a note via mail. It's appreciated more than you realize.

## PROPER USE OF SOCIAL NETWORKS

Social networks like LinkedIn, Facebook, X (formerly Twitter), Instagram, Alignable, and others are tools to use to connect in a personal and professional way with different people in your industry. For me, LinkedIn is a great network to use to reach out to colleagues and get introduced to new contacts. I find, too, that LinkedIn can be an effective professional database to find new people who are like-minded or work in your industry.

It's important to remember that there must be mutual benefit. If you benefit more than the other person in a social network interaction, he or she might feel the relationship is not worth their time and unfollow or "ghost" you as a contact. People have good radar and don't like "being networked." Nobody likes the idea of making a contact with someone and there being an underlying expectation of "you do something for me, and I do something for you." That just feels so contrived.

## MAKE FRIENDS, NOT CONTACTS

I always develop my network as a circle of friends. I refer to this activity as "friend-raising." My contacts become part of my network, and that includes events, activities, business, and personal time. I get to know my contacts personally: What do they like to do? What are their interests? Is there a connection with my own interests? What about their family and their hobbies outside of work?

In my experience, this always leads to long-term relationships and, often, to business that matters. I never expect anything but a good and positive relationship. However, if something comes back to me as a result of the relationship, I am grateful — if not, it doesn't matter, because we are friends.

But if your contact is a friend, someone with whom you are in regular contact, someone with whom you've socialized and connected over a shared interest, then that person will feel much more compelled to help you when you're looking for an opportunity.

By no means is this a suggestion to make friends in the name of getting business — that game is obvious and disingenuous. What I am proposing is that making a good contact and being emotionally genuine pays dividends. The lesson is that when you share your goals, share your aspirations, and share your challenges, there is a rate of return.

## LISTEN

In my thirty-plus years in healthcare as a health administrator, system designer, and healthcare consultant, most of the effort I put forward goes into listening — listening to patients, to the community, to staff, to clients, and to the government.

I've learned that people disclose things when you demonstrate genuine interest in what they're discussing. In my experience, it seems people are used to conversations where others wait for you to finish so they can start talking again. So, when someone actually listens intently to every word, the other person engages better, and more, and eventually they see you as a friend. There's genuine trust established and safety in the relationship. So, listening is not only a learning opportunity but also one of the fastest ways to make friends and build an incredible network. Your friends and network will respect you because you have the patience and maturity to actually listen.

## TELL YOUR PERSONAL STORY

Many people I've met have told me their incredible stories. They are well educated, accomplished, and doing great things. Like most good networkers, I always follow up in a few ways — I send a note to let them know I liked meeting them, I connect with them on LinkedIn, *and* I check them out online. It's my experience that a good online presence tells the world that you walk the walk! In some cases, when I check out a contact's social network profile, I'm disappointed. The story they told me before just doesn't match it. In fact, their profile resembles those of everyone else in their space, so their online story is just boilerplate — nothing jumps out to me that modifies the great individual I encountered in person.

My lesson here is this: Tell your story online, too. Make your online profile match the great story you have! You might think this advice is kitschy or "old school" or even uncool — not so. You might also think telling a good story online does not resonate — also not so. On the contrary, when the story you detail, accurately and genuinely, demonstrates your best traits and is not some boilerplate drivel, it *will* make you stand out. I guarantee it.

## ASK FOR AN INTRODUCTION

I've used my network of contacts for years; it's a well-honed and well-used database. One use is to seek introductions to appropriate people who are either in need of help or who can help me in my business. I always engage my network for introductions, and in my opinion this is often an underused way of meeting new people.

Truth is, everybody knows someone. If you want to meet someone in particular, ask the people in your network if they know anyone who knows the person or someone close to them, and then ask your contact to make an introduction. One of my good friends, Lee Harrison, a businessman in Toronto, is a master at this. There isn't a week that goes by when he doesn't send me a note asking me to introduce him to one of my contacts, or vice versa. I have met many dozens of new people through Lee's seeking introductions to my contacts.

In Lee's case, I always get a follow-up note — "Hey Marc, this is a friend of a friend of a friend, and I think you two should meet." It's so much more effective for my business than a cold call.

That noted, it's important that when you seek introductions this way, you don't over-ask. The best advice here is to use the Lee Harrison file and reciprocate whenever possible. If you want to take advantage of other people's networks, it's on you to build your own network, too. You can't constantly ask for introductions if you don't have something of equal value to share — I learned this over the past forty years. Another lesson here: Build your own network so that when you ask for an introduction, the person you're asking feels comfortable doing so because it's reciprocated.

## GIVE, GIVE MORE – AND THEN ASK

We are in a TikTok-Instagram-YouTube culture where hacks of all varieties are available to apparently help make life easier. Here's a network hack worthy of note — when networking, *give* a dozen times more than asking.

One of my close friends and business colleagues is Bill Thomson, the founder of an investment bank in Toronto. I've known Bill for almost forty years, and he is the consummate networker. I learned two things from him: Whenever someone asks to have lunch or breakfast with you, say yes. You never know where it could lead. And secondly, when meeting someone your first thought should be, "How can I help this person?"

Whenever you help someone reach a goal, make a connection, or overcome an obstacle, like Bill does, you establish an importance to the relationship. It may or may not turn out to be a great friendship, but helping them at least demonstrates a willingness on your part to invest in that person or relationship. It builds trust and shows the incredible value of your network.

It's my experience that when meeting someone, a different kind of relationship is established when the first thing is an ask. It kind of feels icky and sets a dangerous precedent for the relationship. My advice is to avoid this.

So, to make your relationship valuable and long lasting, give first and then give more. I guarantee that this behaviour will net good things for you in the long term.

## YOUR WORD IS EVERYTHING

Using a network comes with huge responsibility. There are referrals for sure, and that's kind of easy, but then there are *reliable* referrals. No one wants to make an introduction to someone who's not often available. That's not good at all. In this lesson, when using a network or being part of one, you're either in or you're not.

This is the most important tenet — particularly in business. Make one fatal and impressive blunder and the reputational damage is infectious, and that is not good either. I had a forty-five-year relationship with John Turner, who was a great networker, and his greatest advice to me was this: "Your word and reputation is your greatest asset. If you say you're going to do something, do it. If you promise to follow up, you've got to fucking follow up." The same can be said for business: If you're closing on a deal, make sure you can keep your word. Your reputation is on the line.

The litmus test for relationships is that if you are able to do this, then your networking efforts pay dividends. If you're not able to keep your word — especially to a friend in your network — then your efforts will amount to nothing and that leads to an unusable network for you. Pointe finale!

———

I have met some truly incredible people in my life and have built an effective network. It works because these lessons pay off. There are other chapters in this book with equally effective advice on how to network and use your network. Both David and I are pleased to present them to you, and if these lessons work, maybe you can let us know.

As the odd couple of networking, we intend to show you that it is not about taking advantage of anyone. It's really about mutual benefit! The real value of a network is to open up opportunities for you and the people you encounter. If this is your motivation, you will see how expansive and positive your friend-raising will become. And when your circle of friends sees that your genuine self and your real story is out there, you will attract what you need.

**Marc Kealey** is chief advocate and founder of Kealey and Associates Inc., a public policy and project management firm serving organizations in Canada and abroad. In this role, he has been instrumental in crafting significant regulations and public policy in Canada. An adviser to former prime minister John N. Turner, Marc is a leading voice for transformation in healthcare, energy, and gaming.

From 2004 to 2007, Marc was the CEO of the largest pharmacy organization in Canada, steering it through the toughest issues of the day, including the *Transparent Drug System for Patients Act*. Prior to 2004, Marc served as GM of Atomic Energy of Canada Ltd. (AECL) and was part of the corporation's CANDU technology team in China and Eastern Europe. From 1990 to 1999, he served as a senior executive at Whitby General Hospital, leading its transition from a community hospital to part of a regional system now known as Lakeridge Health System. He currently sits on several boards and is frequently invited to speak at conferences and to media throughout Canada and globally.

# NO ONE CAN WHISTLE A SYMPHONY –
# IT TAKES AN ORCHESTRA

### Rita Davies | Former Chair of the Ontario Arts Council

We were seated in the mayor's impressive city hall office, with its wall-to-wall, ceiling-to-floor windows overlooking Nathan Phillips Square.

"I never knew I was an artist until I met Ms. Davies. I thought artists were ballerinas, not someone like me from Jamaica."

The speaker was a reggae musician who had come to city hall with his bandmates to meet with then-mayor Art Eggleton.

Back then, in the late 1980s, I headed up the Toronto Arts Council (TAC) and was engaged in a new form of networking: reaching out beyond ballerinas to artists who came from cultures and art traditions we hadn't previously funded or recognized. You might call this the network of inclusion.

This journey of bringing the margins to the mainstream meant I needed to go and meet with individuals and communities who hadn't crossed my path at the TAC and who weren't applying to us. I wanted to find out why.

To do this, I had to get outside of my comfort zone, leave my office, and meet with artists on their turf: I sat in their kitchens and went to backyard barbecues where dub poets, hip hop and rap artists held centre stage. I attended community events featuring performances of

Kathak, a classical form of Indian dance that hadn't yet made it to our main stages. In bars I heard the music of Africa and the Caribbean, music that became the source of a new Toronto mix. I realized that Toronto was missing out on an enormous talent pool of diverse artists and listened as they explained they didn't think they belonged at the arts council. In other words, they didn't feel included.

I understood how difficult it was for an outsider to get in the door, as I had arrived as a refugee in Canada when I was six. Knowing there even is a door, never mind figuring out how to find it, isn't easy for newcomers. It was up to the TAC to help diverse artists find our door and to walk through it. We redesigned programs to become inclusive, to value diverse voices.

That's how I ended up in the mayor's office, with the reggae artist and his band, sitting in a semi-circle around the mayor while I pitched him on the need for equitable funding for the arts.

I remember Mayor Eggleton, his glasses reflecting the sunlight pouring in from his wall of windows, being moved at hearing the stories of each of the musicians, many of whom had come to Canada as children and grew up in economically challenged households.

The musicians, perhaps for the first time, saw themselves as valued by our municipal political leadership. They gained credibility and an understanding that even a poor immigrant kid could come and meet with the mayor of Canada's largest city.

The mayor, for his part, was given a view of how, despite their challenges, kids who picked up a guitar could have their lives transformed by the arts. This was a two-way exchange between the mayor and the musicians where both sides received something of value — a key to successful networking.

"The arts are not something for the narrow elite," Mayor Eggleton later stated, "but vitally important for the mainstream." He learned this lesson that afternoon speaking with the reggae musicians in his office.

———

My path took me from an early interest in theatre to heading the Toronto Arts Council and later the City of Toronto's Culture Office. It was a great learning ground.

I had the good fortune to meet prominent cultural, political, and business leaders along with many, many wonderful artists. These were the crème de la crème of networkers. They each had something to teach me.

Artists like the current City of Toronto Poet Laureate, Lillian Allen, introduced me to young, aspiring talent who found it hard to get through the doors of the establishment. Together, we helped connect many of those young artists to a network of support. They took it from there. Artists like Jully Black and Kardinal Offishall went on to make their own fabulous connections and have storied careers.

From that time, I learned some networking lessons: Don't stick to your lane. Reach out to find the right guides to worlds that intersect with your interests and passions. You never know when a connection that doesn't look like one you need today will be the right one tomorrow. When I first started out to build the resources of the Toronto Arts Council, one of my first steps was to get to know the city politicians who controlled the purse strings. I had no experience or knowledge of the city hall labyrinth. Someone suggested I contact the historian and former city alderman William Kilbourn, who became a great friend to me and the TAC. Bill introduced me around city hall and demystified what at first seemed like an impossible maze.

I realized I also needed to expand my understanding of how artists act as city builders, what role they played in a city's social and economic development. Playwright and theatre founder Tom Hendry, who had worked as an advocate to preserve local neighbourhoods, included me in his neighbourhood and arts circles. Through him I met Jane Jacobs, the world-famous expert on cities. They taught me to bring politics, community, and culture together, which proved to be a powerful combination of networks.

Later, when I worked with Peter Herrndorf, the renowned broadcaster, publisher, and head of the National Arts Centre, to start up the Toronto Arts Awards, he initiated me into the world of arts benefactors from the business and private philanthropic worlds. Two chairs of the Toronto Arts Council, the arts donor Margo Bindhardt and the writer and publisher Anne Collins, included me in their social and professional circles. These are just a few examples of how I was helped by so many generous individuals. I have tried to pay back this generosity over the years with young, aspiring artists and arts workers, for whom I always make time.

It takes patience to grow a network. Getting city politicians on side meant not only formal meetings in their offices but also going out with them to plays and concerts. After the shows, we dropped in backstage. It was the first time many of the politicians had been to an arts event or met an artist. And it was the first time that most of the artists had met a politician.

———

When I first started getting to know the city politicians who controlled the purse strings, they talked and I listened.

"The city budget is tight," I was told. "You need to help me justify putting money into the arts."

We developed a report, *Cultural Capital*, that did just that but still met with resistance.

Another city councillor gave me more advice. "We all get a lot of calls about parking," she said. "Never about an arts issue. You need to change that if you want us to pay attention."

It was time for the artists of Toronto to engage in a form of networking I'll call advocacy. City council was deluged with letters, phone calls, and, most importantly, visits from artists. Today, social media provides an amazing platform for networking and advocacy. But nothing will ever beat the power of face-to-face meetings to develop a network, to pitch your story.

———

I've been describing my experience of networking that pushed for an arts agenda. But what about the artists themselves?

To go back to the title of this chapter: "No one can whistle a symphony. It takes an orchestra to play it," wrote Halford E. Luccock, an early twentieth-century professor. Whether it's an orchestra of 120 players, a theatre production, or a community mural project, the arts thrive on collaboration. The Greeks coined a word that sums this up. It combined "syn," meaning together, and "ergos," meaning work, to get "synergy" — working together or collaborating.

Collaboration is at the heart of many artists' work. Think of all the credits rolling at the end of a film or in a theatre or exhibition program. Think about how many players it takes to bring a symphony to life.

You might assume that coming from a sector where collaboration is so important, artists would be natural networkers. It's a similar skill set: making personal contacts, seeking insight, finding a mentor, interacting on an intuitive as well as practical basis.

But in the arts, as in other sectors, there is both a fear of networking (I'm too shy) and a belief that it's not necessary (what about talent and hard work?).

Let me address how important networking is to success in the arts. Talent and hard work are givens, but they do not guarantee success without networking. Artists must network if they are to succeed. Because getting that gig, landing that part, or securing that exhibition is what makes the difference between great artists and great *successful* artists. Successful artists network.

This isn't just my opinion, though it is something I have noted over the years. This observation, reported in an issue of *Science* magazine, confirmed the importance of networks in the arts to artists' success. These networks may not always be visible, but the intersection of talent with connection was shown to be a vital combination leading to success in arts careers.

As for the awkwardness of meeting total strangers, here's how one veteran arts leader put it to me recently: "You have to put yourself out there, even when it's not comfortable. Refine your pitch. When I ask someone what their project is about, I'll tune out if they can't tell me in a few sentences that grab my attention."

Let's make this my first networking tip:

## Pitch Perfect

Spend time working out that perfect pitch describing who you are and what you are passionate about. Work on your story so that it's succinct, engaging, and will leave your new friend wanting to know more.

Vary your pitch. Politicians and funders may have different objectives, as will a film or theatre producer. Practise speaking it aloud. Getting your story right will help you get over the first awkward moments. I know this has worked for me.

## A Virtuous Cycle

Networking is a process that never ends. Like a garden, it needs constant nurturing. If someone takes time to meet with you, send a note thanking them. Make sure you're as supportive of their career as they are of yours. Take a genuine interest. Comment on their successes. Follow up with an invitation for a coffee. Or, if it makes more sense, get connected on social media.

## Be Authentic

Networking is not about impressing people. Networking in an authentic way is about making friends, not contacts. Don't just talk — *listen*. Forging relationships means engaging in genuine conversations without worrying about how this might help you. It takes time to develop a genuine relationship. Remember the lesson above: Follow up, send a note, nurture these relationships.

## Leave Your Comfort Zone

It's amazing how many people I think of as consummate networkers say this is not their comfort zone. Even the co-editor of this book, David Tsubouchi, has said he's an introvert and must push himself to get out there. I feel the same way and so do many of my colleagues. So, push past the inevitable awkwardness that can come from introducing yourself to a stranger. Accept that invitation. Get out to events in your field. It may never feel quite comfortable, but your reward is that you will expand your growth zone.

## Prepare

Depending on your field, look into organizations and activities that align with your area of work or interest. If relevant, join groups or organizations that will present you with networking opportunities. Find out where you can go to meet people you would like to work with.

Prepare yourself before attending by researching who will be present, who you're interested in meeting. Get to know something about them.

## Social Media

Even though I worked for most of my career in a time before social media, I realize how much could have been achieved if we'd had the tools that are now available. Today's generation of artists and arts workers understands the power of connecting and uses all the available platforms, adapting quickly as new ones evolve.

## Ripple Effect

Finally, I urge you to think about the ripple effects of your networking as you find ways not just to receive help in your career, but to help others. Always be ready to give a hand. Paying it back is your payback. Like I said, it's a virtuous circle. Because no one person can whistle a symphony. It takes a network.

**Rita Davies**, CM, is the former chair of the Ontario Arts Council. She also led Toronto's cultural growth for more than a dozen years as head of culture for the City of Toronto and, before that, at the Toronto Arts Council, where she was known for spearheading diverse and inclusive programs. During her tenure at the city, she oversaw many initiatives, including the development of a first-ever culture plan, the establishment of the wildly successful Nuit Blanche annual festival, and the first major increase in the city's support of the arts in more than a decade. Rita is completing a family memoir, *The Girl from Shanghai*.

# NETWORKING VS. VOLUNTEERING

### Rita Smith | Owner of Rita Smith Enterprises . . . positively inspired communication™

"**Y**ou only take to Heaven what you gave away," my dad used to say. I could update that by saying, "The business you generate develops from the time that you donate."

Forty years ago when I launched my business — Rita Smith Enterprises . . . positively inspired communication™ — I sold my first piece of writing to the *Toronto Star*. It was a humour piece about being a new parent. I mailed it to the editor and they bought it. I was surprised and delighted!

Over the next few years, the *Star* published quite a few of my columns, and having these published tear sheets helped me a lot in seeking other work.

I found a small local paper, the *West Toronto Journal*, which was impressed with my *Star* work and began assigning me events to cover and articles to write. That was harder work, but very exciting.

As it turned out, the owner of the *Journal* also published a trade paper for the taxi industry, *Taxi News*. I went to work for *Taxi News* and never looked back. I was a reporter, then assistant editor, then editor. It was at *Taxi News* that I learned how to do graphic layout, a skill I have never stopped using.

The owner of *Taxi News* was a committed political activist and referred me to the first politician for whom I ever wrote. I did not keep him long as a client; I found him to be dishonest and sneaky. However, the experience made me realize I had a flair for political writing and communications strategy, two skills I've sold for decades afterward.

———

Computers — first with modems, and later the internet — quickly changed the way professionals solicited and delivered work. However, even with the fastest digital technologies at our fingertips, everyone in communications and virtually every other form of personal services will tell you that while they might *deliver* paying projects using the internet, they meet, impress, and get to know their best and biggest customers by meeting them in person . . . somewhere. But where?

I attended bluntly branded "networking sessions" a few times. Sometimes there was food and drink, and at other times it was just a room full of people with a new or small business milling around, looking awkward and lost. Everyone had a giant name tag, and occasionally, I met an interesting conversationalist. Never once, however, did I get hired to write by anyone I met at a "networking session." That's okay, though, because I discovered early on where all the paying customers were: in the groups where I volunteered.

## PEOPLE SEE YOU AT YOUR BEST

My church newsletter, our computer user group, community groups, business associations, and sporting leagues all turned out to be packed full of people who announced they needed something *else* done at almost every meeting.

"I have to write a newsletter at my job — can I pay you to help?" Or "We need someone to create a flyer for the business association sidewalk sale — can I hire you to help?"

When you volunteer for a worthy cause, I learned, potential clients sitting around the table really see you at your very best, full of enthusiasm and passion. No one was ever awkward or shy at these meetings; they weren't there to network. They were there to get an important job done. I was there to help them do that because I believed what they were doing mattered. We were all at our best, working with shared purpose and objectives.

## PROOF YOU CAN DO THE WORK

Quickly, my portfolio of published tear sheets grew thick and fat. Whether I was paid to write them or not, they were crucial in helping me win *real* contracts at serious money.

One day, an agency with which I was registered called to tell me Hewlett-Packard had contacted them to inquire about hiring a writer.

"There are prerequisites," Barb told me nervously. "The writer has to have computer tear sheets."

"I've got a pile of them," I assured her, and sent over several of the most recent computer user group newsletters in which I was credited as the writer. That HP contract paid my bills for several years, and got me a contract with Sony, too.

My local business association turned out to be an even more lucrative contract scenario than all the technology writing I ever did. Originally, the group hired me to deliver a monthly newsletter, which quickly turned into a full annual contract for all kinds of promotions.

## THE BOTTOMLESS PIT OF WORK

That business association, founded by the minister of a local church and later supported by 120 businesses, was the ultimate networking stepping stone, as it led me to the bottomless pit of work for a writer: politics.

Through this community group, I met our local mayor; I volunteered on his election campaigns. He became a member of Provincial Parliament and hired me as his press secretary, which launched the political writing career that is still paying off to this day.

As a political volunteer, I saw that people from a multitude of industries join political groups to both support a good candidate and to meet people. Accountants, car dealers, communications professionals, property managers, artists and musicians, insurance agents — I have seen them all use politics to network successfully over the years. My favourite was a funeral director who served on his local business association as a way of meeting folks who would eventually need to be buried — and he was right!

## NEW TECHNOLOGIES

An additional benefit of volunteering with a variety of groups is learning new technologies. As an individual, I couldn't or wouldn't choose to invest in all the latest, greatest products or processes. As a volunteer, I was trained on computer applications, tools, and technologies I didn't even know existed before someone handed them to me and asked me to get a job done.

Some of these groups also sent me on amazing training courses — leadership, team building, database building, time management, and planning. Once you have those skills, you never stop using them to improve your business.

The newest trend in technology, which only *seems* like bad news for writers, is artificial intelligence (AI).

With the advent of AI in the content-creating world, it may seem like writers are no longer needed. Nothing could be further from the truth! Yes, at times an AI program may be useful in generating some text. I've used it to save time researching background. However, so long as the original story idea comes from my brain or the primary-source information is as a result of my work, I have no fear of being replaced by AI.

This is where your hard work networking will be most helpful, because so long as you have information and comments based upon original information gleaned from real human beings, you won't be easily replaced.

For example, when I write an article based on an interview I have done with an industry leader, no other writer or any AI program can provide that exact news and information before I publish it. Later, AI can scrape the internet, find my article and refer to it, but until I discover the information, quote the expert, write the story, and publish it, it is not available anywhere, least of all to an AI program.

So long as you stay on top of networking, build up your contacts list, and become a subject matter expert or specialist in the industries about which you hope to write, you cannot be replaced by artificial intelligence.

## ACCIDENTALLY EARNING MONEY

I found volunteering as a networking and marketing method so effective, I actually had to rethink the process and remember that I *used* to volunteer because I believed in the causes, not because I was hoping to ambush attendees and make money. So, when I wound up volunteering for my own church, I promised myself that no matter what occurred, I would not use the group to make money.

The priests were ecstatic to have someone around to help them with newsletter writing, and after a period of time, Father John shyly asked if I might try my hand at ghostwriting his weekly column, "From the Pastor's Desk."

"I know this is my job; I am supposed to write it," he said nervously, "but honestly, I just run out of ideas. Every day is so busy. When I sit down to write it, my brain goes blank, and I can't write a word."

Networking vs. Volunteering | 95

"Well, let me have a run at it," I suggested. "This is brand new to me. I've never tried it before."

I began a series of weekly columns based on that week's Gospel reading, and because I was so new at it, they were completely original. Father John was torn between delight with having exciting new columns and terror at anyone finding out he had hired a ghostwriter to "minister to his flock."

"It will be our secret," I promised him. "I will never tell anyone."

A few months went by before he called me in an absolute panic: "Rita, the *Catholic Register* just called me!" he stuttered in terror. "Apparently, one of their editors attends our church and told them that our newsletter runs the most interesting Pastor's columns . . . they want me to write some columns for them!"

I could not help but laugh at the irony. "Do you want me to write them?"

"No, I can't lie," he said. "I can't lie about the columns, and I won't lie to the *Catholic Register*. I am going to tell them you write the columns and give them your phone number."

So as the story ended, I did write the columns for the *Catholic Register*, and they insisted on paying me.

"Wow," I had to laugh when we finished talking about the money. "Even when I try to give it away for free, it turns into money."

## BUILD IT INTO YOUR SCHEDULE

Perhaps the most structured and productive period during which I used volunteering as a marketing technique was during one of Ontario's worst recessions. I lost several clients and realized that I had only about thirty hours sold every week.

"Well, I'm not going to work less than forty hours per week, minimum," I resolved. "I'll find a group to give the ten hours to."

I lived up to my commitment and never worked less than forty hours per week, whether I was being paid or not. These volunteer hours, as they always had previously, were like the yeast in a rising loaf of bread: My network of contacts expanded and exploded until by the end of the year, I had sold every waking hour I had for good money again.

## IT'S NOT WHO YOU KNOW

I had already been putting my "don't network, volunteer" strategy to work for many years before I heard from a young man who was a recent immigrant to Canada. He had been working very, very hard to find paying projects and called me full of disgust and dismay after hearing that a friend had been hired by someone in local government.

"It's true!" he exclaimed angrily. "In Canada, it's not what you know, it's who you know!"

I did not hesitate to think but replied instantly: "It's not who you *know*, Sam. It's who you *come through for*.

"No one, in any industry, is going to hire you just because they know you. They might hire you if you have come through for them in the past, in a pinch, when they had no budget or when there was no one else to turn to for help. I don't get referred by strangers; neither does your friend. He came through for someone, somewhere. Get out there and get busy delivering for someone who needs help. Paid work will follow."

He did, and it did.

## SUMMARY

1. When you are volunteering, people see you at your enthusiastic best. It's a great advertisement for the professional you.
2. The group itself probably does not have the budget to pay you — but individual members come from all kinds of industries, and *they* have the budget.

3. Volunteering is a great way to learn and stay up to date on technologies, tools, and professional processes.
4. Don't sit around sulking when you could be volunteering. Go make yourself useful! It will turn into money eventually. If it doesn't, you will make new friends.
5. It's not who you know; it's who you come through for.
6. You only take to Heaven what you gave away.

**Rita Smith** has been a writer for forty years, published in the *Toronto Star*, *Globe and Mail*, and *Toronto Sun*, and is a regular contributor to *True North*. She has delivered internal and external communications planning, stakeholder management, and media relations for clients in the private and public sectors and several non-profit organizations, and she has managed extensive earned, paid, and social media campaigns. Rita is the editor and publisher of *Taxi News* and *Road Warrior News*.

# THE JOY OF NETWORKING

### Susan Murray | Founder and CEO of
### S.A. Murray Consulting Inc.

I had the privilege of meeting David Tsubouchi in the late 1990s when he was a member of Ontario premier Mike Harris's cabinet. We reconnected through LinkedIn and our mutual involvement in the Canadian pension industry.

Marc Kealey and his partner Daniela are long-time friends. We met through our very dear mutual friend, the late John Turner.

In many ways, we three share similar professional histories. A decades-long involvement with Canadian politics, volunteer work, and for Marc and me, a shared history growing up in similar "blue-collar" cities in Ontario. Marc in Niagara Falls and me in "The Hammer" — Hamilton. Both cities were and continue to be settled by waves of immigrants, from the eighteenth century to today. As an adult, I recognized early on that it was a privilege to grow up in a melting-pot city. Many of my high school friends of all backgrounds worked in the steel mills for the summers.

Today, Hamilton remains a manufacturing city, but it has diversified with major medical research centres, become a university and college town with a thriving art and music scene, and has the sixth-largest public art gallery in Canada, the Art Gallery of Hamilton.

David and I share the introvert gene. It took energy, discipline, and focus for me to become an extrovert. Our friend Marc is the Energizer Bunny — he never stops and is an extraordinary networker and entrepreneur.

———

A significant part of my life has been and remains volunteer work. A lifetime of volunteer work that I began in high school has cascaded over the years from local to national and international non-profits.

These connections from giving back and paying it forward have so enriched my life. The resulting reward becomes the creation of a network of friends and business associates.

My journey into public life began in my first year at Western University in London, Ontario. I was approached to run for the Social Science seat on the student council. That single decision changed the trajectory of my life and career.

As our family dinners involved debates and proving your positions, I was comfortable selling myself and, once elected, became a very active member of council. In my second year, I was elected the first student senator and, in my fourth year, the first student governor to sit on the University Board of Governors.

Western's senate was made up of tenured professors and very insular. The London press reported on every meeting. The key issue I worked on for months with the only woman dean, and then presented to a senate meeting, was a set of recommendations for better safety on campus, particularly for female students. For example, much better lighting at night as it is a very large campus with many paths between classes and residences.

Our report got a lot of coverage on radio and in newspapers. Also in attendance at these meetings were the senior administrators and president.

Within twenty-four hours of the story breaking, I was called into the president's office. My academic records had been pulled and I was

The Joy of Networking | 101

left to stand while the four most senior men at Western humiliated and berated me for going public, to quote: "How dare you embarrass the university." That was an early lesson in abuse of power!

———

At Western, I came to the attention of the Young Progressive Conservatives — the YPC. I was invited to speak to the club about how to attract fellow students to it. I accepted, and met John Tory, who was president of the Ontario YPC, and some of London's prominent elected provincial PCs, both cabinet ministers and MPPs.

It was at this time that my father introduced me to his closest friend, Tom Scott, head of the creative department for the national advertising firm Foster Advertising, which was headquartered in Toronto and then the largest ad firm in Canada. Tom was the youngest member of Premier Bill Davis's Blue Machine — then the most powerful and successful political team in the country.

Mr. Scott became my mentor and facilitator at Queen's Park, introducing me to Government Members Services, which became my first full-time position. It was an exciting time to be working in a legislature and meeting so many talented young political staffers. Many remain lifelong friends and went on to their own elected careers, among them former Ontario finance minister Janet Ecker, MPP for Oakville North Effie Triantafilopoulos, and a parliamentary secretary in Premier Doug Ford's government.

My political commitment led me to run for fifth vice-president of the Ontario PC party against incumbent Pauline Browes. I won, and Pauline is both a friend and had her own distinguished federal political career.

Early female trail-breakers in the Davis cabinet, like Bette Stephenson and Margaret Birch, helped to get young female Conservatives into the now only reworking political club left in Canada: the 140-year-old Albany Club, the first private club to admit women in Canada.

For us under-thirty members, what a privilege it was to network with older members. One of my favourite memories — as none of us owned a car — was a few of us being driven to an event by Hal Jackman, a powerful businessman who owned and controlled many prominent businesses such as Empire Life and Dominion Insurance.

It was raining, and I was in the front seat. My feet started to get wet, and I saw there was almost no floor as it had rusted out. I asked Mr. Jackman why he did not buy a new car, and he sternly answered: "Because a car is a wasting asset!"

———

It was working at Queen's Park, interacting with businesses and non-profit organizations, that sparked the idea of the business I founded at age 28: S.A. Murray Consulting Inc., or SAMCI as it became known.

Was it jumping off a cliff? Yes, as I had no business experience or network. I spent months making cold calls to companies I believed could use my services. My first client came through just such a call to the president of Canadian-owned and managed Massey Ferguson, then the largest farm equipment maker in the world. They were in a precarious financial situation and agreed to meet.

That journey to save the company was long and complicated, and the approvals had to be ratified by both the Ontario and federal governments. We were successful and that launched my company.

Our SAMCI team worked with all provincial and federal governments for over thirty years. That led us to making lifelong friends and colleagues in all parties. Many of my former clients and employees who remain in Canada, the U.S., and Europe are part of my network of friends.

Taking on new challenges is exciting. Years ago, the head of national corporate affairs at CIBC strongly believed the bank should be offering start-up loans to start-ups owned by women. That led me to working with my client Bill Neville to create a two-day conference called Women in Power. We held it in Toronto, and it was a sellout. Some of the women who attended received funding and today still run successful businesses.

The Joy of Networking | 103

———

To return to giving back, I strongly recommend volunteer work to build fellowship and friendships and enjoy lifelong learning. Many of the volunteer boards that I have served on have created some of my most lasting friendships.

Volunteer and career work go hand in hand with networking. Those connections led me directly to the privilege of sitting on three public corporate boards and three private ones.

Good to great networkers are endlessly curious and therefore delighted to meet and connect with new people. Equally gratifying is connecting and interacting in a positive way every day with everyone we meet in our daily travels. Today, we have incredible tools such as LinkedIn to assist us to quickly build our networks.

So why did I title my chapter the joy of networking? The answer is simple: If we smile and connect, respect, and talk to all who cross our paths every day and make just one person's day, that is joyful.

**Susan A. Murray** is the founder and CEO of S.A. Murray Consulting Inc. (SAMCI). She is the first woman to found and build a national government relations firm. SAMCI's reputation has been built on providing counsel and direct activities to optimize relationships between provincial, federal, private, and non-profit companies and national charities.

Susan led the parliamentary discussions in Ottawa to bring transparency in disclosing public and private interests and was deeply involved in creating the first national lobbying legislation.

# WHY A NON-LINEAR PATH TO NETWORKING?

### Stephen Brickell | President and CEO of
### Fusion Universal Healthcare

Networking? What is the purpose? How do you measure your return on investment for your time, resources, and reputation?

When my very good friend David Tsubouchi asked me to contribute a chapter to his book exploring the diverse approaches to personal networking, I was curious to see the dichotomy of these styles. Most people like and understand the certainty of a definite linear formula — if you do X and Y, it will result in Z. However, the successful networkers I have observed follow a non-linear path best described as a formula of art and science.

The best example I have ever observed is David and his unique approach to networking. The way David operates reminds me of a scene from the movie *The Godfather*: When the Godfather calls you and asks for a favour, the answer is always yes, primarily out of fear. With David, my answer is always yes, but not out of fear. When he asks for a favour, it will come from a place to help others, with the end result providing little to no personal benefit to himself. David is the best example of a "pay it forward" type of individual, or as *New York Times* bestselling author Adam Grant would call it, a "giver."

As a Canadian, I must first apologize for this chapter. Some of you will likely have a hard time understanding the lens that I see the world through. My educational background in engineering and business, coupled with thirty-five years at a little computer company, IBM, resulted in my brain being wired to a systems approach and its corresponding methodologies. I love studying repeatable activities, monitoring for output success, and continuously modifying with evidence-based data (sorry to geek out). For a few of you, this will resonate and hopefully open your aperture to view new networking approaches. It may not for others, but I challenge you to understand the thought process behind this. While you may not utilize any of it, it may help provide some insight and empathy towards how others see the world, making the process we call networking more effective and enjoyable for all. Wow, a win-win.

## STEPHEN'S SIX-STEP METHODOLOGY TO NETWORKING

1. Why
2. Quantity or Quality?
3. Be Ready for Surprises
4. Quest for Diversity
5. Be Inclusive
6. If You Are Not Having Fun, You Are Doing It Wrong

Fun fact: What is a methodology? The Wikipedia definition says: "In its most common sense, methodology is the study of research methods. However, the term can also refer to the methods themselves or to the philosophical discussion of associated background assumptions."[*]

So, my lifetime of research/observation into networking styles and patterns grew my six-step methodology.

---

\* "Methodology," Wikipedia, May 26, 2024, https://en.wikipedia.org/wiki/Methodology.

Why a Non-Linear Path to Networking? | 107

# 1. WHY

When we were five, we learned to question everything. Yes, it drove our parents crazy, but in the innocence of understanding *why*, we are doing something very powerful. What is the outcome you want? Are you using the network for self-benefit or altruistically to help others? The answer could be a yes to one of those or a hybrid, depending on the situation.

You should question why knowing your "why" is so important. Is this an unnecessary step? A waste of time? I just want to gain a network of people to help me achieve my goal, you might say. But depending on what your goal is, you may not be populating your network with the right people. Why would people want to be part of your network? Why would they have an interest in helping you?

One of my favourite authors is Simon Sinek, and his book *Start with Why* became a *New York Times* bestseller. His TED Talk derived from that book has created a massive following, with over 64 million views.

To understand how "why" is important, Sinek masterfully simplifies his evidence-based findings. He uses the concept of the golden circle. His observation is that people are inspired by *why* you are doing something, and then *how* you do it, followed by *what* you are doing. This hierarchy or order of operations is critical to effectiveness and success in nearly all avenues of life.

So why am I promoting this leadership book, and how does it have a relationship to my six-step networking methodology?

Think about people in your current network. Do you know their "why"? When they ask for your help, or when you ask them for help, does knowing the "why" factor into a yes? What is the energy level and commitment to those who know their "why"? Even if it is not aligned with your "why," your understanding and respect of their "why" determines your engagement to support their success. In your network, name the top three people who articulate their "why." Now, think about three people in your network whose "why" you have no clue about. Rate your observation of how you and others help them achieve their goals.

108 | The Ripple Effect

I would like to introduce additional depth to "why." In your network, of the ones who do identify a "why," are they a "giver" or a "taker"?

One of my other favourite authors is behavioural psychologist Adam Grant. Grant, like Sinek, is a *New York Times* bestselling author. Both provide thought-provoking, evidence-based research into human interaction. Grant's book *Give and Take* is a detailed, research-backed observation of team (network) dynamics and the effectiveness of groups and what they are able to achieve.

Think about the people you work with on a daily basis. If I asked you to categorize them by the statements "the world revolves around me" or "how will this impact me," it's likely you could think of a few individuals. Congratulations, you have found the "takers"!

Now let's try this again. Can anyone you work with be characterized by the following: "I can always rely on them," "They are willing to help without expectation of reciprocity," and "I feel this person wants to see me succeed"? If so, you have found the "givers." In his global research involving thirty thousand people, Grant found that a team of "givers" outperforms "takers." Adam Grant's TED Talk is one of my favourites, with over ten million views. I would suggest that investing thirteen minutes in it is well worth your time and will help you understand the context of its impact on networking. It may in fact change your life.

Now, think about your "why" and those in your network. Those who present a "why" and can be identified as "givers," in my experience, have an exponentially higher level of effectiveness in leveraging their network.

Here's a fun side fact about applying Adam Grant's TED Talk. One of my volunteer activities is being the director of a sailing school. At Whitby Yacht Club, I did a hostile takeover of a volunteer position (yes, a new level of crazy). The club's not-for-profit summer sail camp was losing a lot of money, attendance was in free fall, and the quality of the program was as bad as you could imagine. My first summer, I did not hire any of the previous instructors back and started the rebuilding with a culture based on three principles: one, safety; two, fun (if the kids are not having fun, the effectiveness of learning is reduced); and three, increase their confidence, skill, and sailing ability. We focused on hiring the Adam Grant "givers." During interviews, we specifically looked for "giver" traits. After hiring, we had them watch Grant's TED Talk. At the orientation, we watched it again, and I explained we worked hard to only hire "givers," so this would be a trusted, safe place for you to be a 100 percent giver. I also told them that if they were a "taker" and fooled us during the interview, to please try to be a "giver" for the eight-week summer camp and see how their life could be different. If not, then this is not the right place for them, and without hesitation, I will fire them! The truth is the availability of qualified sailing instructors is tight, and we hired some "takers" because we had no other choice.

The result? With this focus on "giver" culture, in the first three years, attendance grew by a compounded 100 percent year over year. All instructors who had not graduated from their schooling returned each year. On a ten-year metric, our eight-week summer revenue grew from $14k to over $300k, while instructor staffing grew from four to twenty-four to support the exponential enrollment growth. Most importantly, our participant and parent satisfaction surveys are near 100 percent in all categories. Imagine the challenge of ramping an annual eight-week company with twenty-four employees with little to no work experience (high school, college, or university students) into what would be a company with $2.4 million in annualized revenue and extremely high customer satisfaction? Not that hard if you have a team of "givers."

## 2. QUANTITY OR QUALITY?

Quantity or quality is not an either-or question. It is not a right or wrong but more of a situational response to your "why."

In 2023, LinkedIn turned twenty and achieved 922 million global members. To put that in perspective, of those living and working in North America, approximately two out of every three citizens have a LinkedIn account. With that reach and penetration, it should make networking so easy. Create an account and spend a few hours a day creating interesting content that will then be liked by others. If you are fortunate enough to have an opportunity to attend or speak at industry conferences, that number has the potential to grow exponentially. I recall inviting a hospital CIO, and friend, to be a mainstage speaker at an IBM global conference attended by forty thousand people. When he returned home, he had thousands of new requests. The only downside was when his pregnant wife looked over his shoulder and saw the picture of one female requester, she thought LinkedIn was a dating site. I never really thought of the name LinkedIn that way, but I now see her side, and I did get a call that night from him to chat with his wife and verify his story.

In the world of LinkedIn and other social media platforms, quantity is not a challenge. Not to be mistaken, I don't think there is a downside to crafting an expansive LinkedIn network, whether it be one thousand or one hundred thousand, as this provides you with the quantity component of tapping into your "why." But in itself it is not wholly sufficient in generating an effective and meaningful network — you still need to consider the quality component. What is the quality of your network?

Quality networks are the ones that you connect with daily and include people you worked with five years ago who you can reengage with like you last connected yesterday. Or people that once a month or once a year you make the time to have a coffee, breakfast, or lunch with. Now think about the quality person that you may not have kept up with but wished you had. Here's a task for you: Make a list of your network and divide it into an A and a B section. A's are the closest to you — you work with them daily, or you are able to pick up where you left off, regardless of how long it has been since your last contact. B's are the ones you have lost some contact with, which can occur for a variety of reasons. In that B list, identify a few key people that you have lost contact with and make a plan to reach out to them. You can either schedule this in your calendar or it can be impromptu call when you are stuck in traffic. Call them up and say, "I miss talking to you, what's happening in your world?" Make it an authentic conversation and make it about them. Ask if there is anything you can do to help them. If it is not obvious, ask them their "why." In my experience, it will make their day better because you were thinking about them and asking how you could help for nothing in return. It will also improve your day and energize your network. Give it a try, what do you have to lose?

Side note: The reason for approaches, either scheduled or while stuck in traffic, is to help keep yourself accountable on networking and to show that it doesn't need to be an extensively planned event. It is easy to justify why you have not kept in contact with them — not enough time in the day, too many pre-existing obligations, etc. I like to lead with a "Sorry we have not talked in a while." Most people do not understand that saying "Sorry" is one of the most self-empowering forms of networking communication. It positions you to take accountability and control of the situation. It works so much better than "hey, why have you not kept in touch?" This puts the other person on the defensive, and they start thinking, "Now I know why I never kept in touch with you."

It would be just as easy to justify putting these calls off. Make a plan, stick to it, and remember that it isn't an interview, but rather a conversation with an old friend that you want to support. Not only will you feel better, but you also just put a smile on someone's face and made their day better, too. Another win-win.

### 3. BE READY FOR SURPRISES

It may just be me, but I have discovered some of my most rewarding relationships in the least obvious places. Have you ever had a first impression of someone that made you immediately discount the opportunity to network with them? The initial impressions are likely a combination of stereotypes and personal past experiences.

I challenge you to be ready to be wrong. Be ready for new information and continuously reassess previous notions based on new information; I guarantee you will surprise yourself.

## Surprises in action . . .

### David Tsubouchi: Another boring IBM meeting . . . or not?

It was in a stereotypical corporate meeting at IBM. I was leading a solution team working to help a part of government improve their process, better serve the citizens, and reduce cost (this is the time your eyes glaze over and you start nodding off; really, I was). One of my team members invited David to see if he could help us with some connections in his network. My first impression was, okay, an ex-politician who will have limited real interest in what we are doing and is just interested in what is in it for him. Wow, I was so wrong — remember, get excited about being wrong because you are closer to being more right. David's mind became so engrossed in how we could help solve a big problem. Then he switched gears and kicked into his *Beautiful Mind* memory bank, a who's who of people in government that he could call up and introduce me to.

After a private conversation, I thanked him and asked how to repay him. Did he want to send me an invoice for consulting, or what would the compensation for his work look like? He looked at me with what could best be described as bewilderment and insult. He told me he just liked to help people. Up until that point, most of my world had been a combination of "what's in it for me?" or "quid pro quo." David introduced me to a dimension that literally changed my life. I have always been ultra-competitive in sports and business. That left little room or understanding for being a "giver." David's personality is also extreme on the competitive scale, but somehow, somewhere, he developed a "giver" style. It has now been over fifteen years that David and I have been close friends, and he continues to amaze me with the depth of his giving nature. My personal success in business and life benefited from how this relationship evolved my thinking.

Why a Non-Linear Path to Networking? | 113

### *Trina Boivin: A weekend sailing regatta like every other . . . or not?*

All three of our children have been competitive sailors, with the youngest making it to the Ontario provincial sailing team. Like all parents, you spend a lot of time and money travelling around to support them while making small talk to the other parents. I never would have thought that one weekend regatta at the Buffalo Canoe Club would yield a life-changing epiphany.

I knew Trina as the mother of a competitor who was friends with my daughter. In casual conversation, I asked what she did to support her daughter's sailing, which can be expensive. It was interesting that she, like me, had just stepped out of corporate life and was going out on her own and building a company around her interests and expertise. I was intrigued: She had held executive positions, like I had, and was now focused on growing her client base by offering executive coaching, leadership, behaviour assessments, and team effectiveness training. I shared with her that any team or organization that I build must have all three of the legs to my "why" stool. First, I want to make a positive impact on as many people as possible. Second, it is all about the team and being able to work with incredible people in the organization, the partners, and the clients. Third, I want a business model that allows the organization to be sustainable, increase positive impact exponentially with its growth, and reward everyone who gives it their all in making that positive impact on others.

Once she understood and believed my "why," the switch turned on, barriers came down, and it was a magical collaboration. I then shared that the current engagement that was demanding most of my energy was to help improve rural healthcare. As it turned out, a lot of Trina's clients were hospital CEOs and other executives in healthcare. That was the beginning of an amazing, mutually beneficial collaboration.

The second gift I received that weekend was a rapid insight to improve the effectiveness of my own networking ability. I shared with my new BFF, in a very vulnerable way, that although I was humbled by the depth of my working relationships where people believed in the vision and business model, I have an ability to create a strong dislike of me personally.

In one dimension, I am able to create an amazing team that will work unlimited hours with no remuneration, hoping success might come in the future. However, my entire career I have been embarrassed to have a personality that seems to have a Boolean/binary impact on people. I told Trina that people either love working with me, or, for some reason, they develop an instant disdain. With the precision of a sharpshooter, she knew why and hit the target dead centre. It felt like a shot between my eyes. Afterward, she asked me to give examples of the people with whom I have been challenged to develop a relationship, and she gave me a homework assignment that night. Trina assigned me to read a paper by David Rock, "Managing with the Brain in Mind." Neuroscience research is revealing the social nature of the high-performance workplace.

Rock's model identifies how people are internally centred and their threat/reward triggers. They are defined in a five-category model called SCARF:[*]

- **S**tatus: These are people whose status is precious to them and provides them power, which is also their vulnerability.
- **C**ontrol: These people like to feel in control and know what's next, and typically are not comfortable with surprises.
- **A**utonomy: This group wants to have autonomy on how they achieve their goals; they like to be accountable and responsible for results; being micromanaged is their negative trigger.
- **R**elatedness: People who want a sense of belonging to a group and gain comfort in group settings.
- **F**airness: This group wants to live in a fair and just world; they feel that people who do the work deserve the credit.

The next day, after doing my reading homework, Trina assessed me as a person who has a charisma when he enters the room, but because I am an "autonomy" person who cares about results, impacts, and fairness

---

[*] David Rock, "SCARF: A Brain-based Model for Collaborating with and Influencing Others," *NeuroLeadership Journal*, vol. 1, no. 1, December 2008.

towards others, this style threatens some people. The "status" people, who were my conflict group in Trina's assessment, can take a dislike to me because I do not care about what they hold most precious (in full disclosure, I have been known to give a middle finger to status-oriented people). Kidding aside, if I want to increase my networking effectiveness, I have to own up to the negative impact I can have on others who are orientated to areas different than mine. That will take some work.

### FU.healthcare . . . the biggest surprise of all

"No, no, no!"

My dear friend David Tsubouchi was asked by a friend to sit on the board of a small telehealth start-up company. Given he was already overstretched in his time commitments, it was not possible; however, he could not say no and agreed to be an adviser. In turn, he asked me, given my IBM experience in healthcare, to evaluate their business model. My first reaction was "no." I explained to David that telehealth was an overcrowded, low-margin, and questionable method to deliver quality outcomes. Then he said his *Godfather* words: "Could you do it as a favour because I really liked these guys and what they are trying to do is very important" (David's "why"). So, by now, you know my answer had to be yes because it was David, and I respected and trusted his "why."

This group of six medical specialists were trying to support rural family doctors in emergency situations. They were literally helping with life-or-death situations. They were saving lives, but the business model since 2014 was hemorrhaging cash and unsustainable. They had invested a lot of their own money and time with no return. Twice, the technology companies they contracted with underdelivered and overpriced technology apps. Yet in the face of all that adversity they continued because of their "why." There was no option for me to not support this incredible group based on their "why."

In my research, I discovered numerous studies in Canada and globally that reveal that if you live in a rural area, you will die early and have poorer health due to the lack of adequate medical resources.

Rural areas are undersupported by family doctors and medical facilities. Local hospitals do not have the emergency or medical specialist support like urban populations enjoy. After interviewing the founders and some of the rural family doctors they support, I clearly understood their "why." It now became my "why." The biggest problem was that no matter how much I respected this group and their mission, I could not see any way their business model could even provide a break-even financial result to sustain what they were doing.

I dedicated months trying to develop a sustainable business model. During that process, I engaged my network of healthcare, technology, government, and crazy out-of-the-box thinkers to find a way to make a model that could work. It goes without saying that all contributions were on a friend-favour basis since there was no money available, but they respected my "why."

Through my network of extraordinary people, I created my "challenge network." I use this method of dynamically assembling a group for speed and diverse thinking. A challenge network consists of passionate people who are typically subject experts who can approach a problem by respectfully challenging each other to move beyond the problem and the status quo. The net contribution of my challenge network was a business model that had the potential to deliver a financially sustainable output and even support global growth. Our aperture had now expanded to use Canada as our development and testing site.

I then extended my network to ask for free help to develop the technology platform. My "why" to the recruited team was a three-legged stool — if we are successful, the result will be: first, we will help improve the health of people on a global scale and contribute to saving lives; second, we will be working with a group of incredible "givers" and have fun in the process; and third, if we execute the business model, this will provide the funds for global sustainable growth and reward the team.

We started to execute the business model and develop the technical platform in January 2023. Working weekends and evenings, we made progress. Our weekly team scrum calls were 8 p.m., Thursday and Sunday, and sometimes went to 2 a.m. We delivered on our first paid launch in September 2023, supporting sixty-five nurses to provide care for homeless communities. Our second paid launch in October provided emergency support to a remote mining site with one thousand workers. Before our launch, they were evacuating one to two people a day by air because they were not able to assess their condition or provide onsite support. After our implementation, that dropped to one to two a *week* and the site's health outcomes were better overall. From the business side, the mining company was also happy because each evacuation cost $10,000 to $20,000.

So now, after trying to say "no" to my friend, I am all in and the CEO of what we hope will be a transformational movement in global rural healthcare.

The new branded name for this soon-to-be-global project is Fusion Universal Healthcare — Fusion, because like nuclear fusion it is bringing the energy of two elements together for unlimited power (specialist and family doctors), and Universal because we believe that people everywhere deserve good, quality healthcare. In marketing and brand management, you strive for an identifiable brand name that is hard to forget. I dare you to forget the short name FU.healthcare. Beyond the obvious FU reference, in the world of specialist and family doctors, FU is short for "follow up."

Stephen.Brickell@FU.Healthcare — can you forget that name?

In addition to the founding six doctors, I am humbled by my network of friends who selflessly bought into this "why" to help build the technology and execute the business model. I cannot think of a better example to demonstrate the power of knowing and communicating the "why" or building a network team of "givers" than the group we have formed to improve healthcare, on a global scale:

**Our Business Leadership**
Stephen Brickell, Chief Enthusiasm Officer
Neilson Mclean, Chief Medical Innovation Officer
Raj Balasubramanian, Chief Technology Officer
Ervin Forth, Technology Development Director
Peter Brickell, Communication Innovation Director
Andrea Brinston, Legal Counsel

**Our Founding Medical Leadership**
Dr. Don Burke
Dr. Neilson Mclean
Dr. Marietjie Slabbert
Dr. Mario Francispragasam
Dr. James Kung
Dr. Omar Ahmed
Dr. Ishtiaq Ahmed

Lastly, here's my personal formula for being ready for surprises:

1. *Wow*, I am wrong a lot.
2. Get excited by being wrong. When you discover you are wrong, it gets you closer to being more right and that is where the big opportunities are found.
3. Know your "why" and share it to build a committed network of "givers" around you.

## 4. QUEST FOR DIVERSITY

Birds of a feather may flock together, but does that create a network of myopic thinking? Go back to your "why." Do you want a safe place

Why a Non-Linear Path to Networking? | 119

in your network where people share common interests and points of view? Or do you want a challenge network? The answer to both could well be yes. The yin/yang opposites can provide great value to you, and you can provide it to others (be a "giver").

My personal belief is that when you create a network of diversity, in every aspect (work/life experience, race, religion, culture, gender, sexual orientation, educational background, etc.), you have a unique and powerful opportunity.

Is diversity really that important? If your "why"s are consistently a narrow grouping — let's say to support left-handed accountants who have only worked three years, live in a suburban neighbourhood, have been married for four years with one child, Baptist church on Sundays, etc. — you likely do not need diversity input or a challenge network. But I would suggest this is a rare-to-never case.

So how do you design a diverse network? I am often teased by my family and friends about my overuse of spreadsheets, but you may think about doing a networking inventory. Think about categorizing the diversity that will bring you value. Seek out people who can fill those current voids, and remember to observe the SCARF model so you can be effective and empathetic in communication. I find it is best to also uncover their "why" to support their diversity.

## 5. BE INCLUSIVE

You might be thinking, so first you want me to be diverse and now inclusive? My intent is to challenge your thinking and hurt your brain a little. From the previous step, you have expanded your network to represent diversity. It took stretching on your part to embrace alternative ways of seeing the world. Now the highest return on your time investment is when you can create an environment where everyone respectfully comes together. The secret is a common "why" for your team that is bigger than yourselves. This can create the most amazing and impactful challenge network. Challenge networks are a special

120 | The Ripple Effect

place where there is a trust that your network is looking out for your best interest, they will support you when you need it, and will challenge your thoughts and actions when you need it.

Global observation: The respect and the ability to listen to diverse voices seem to be missing. Politics, journalism, and too often personal opinions project myopic statements of good versus evil. There is no room to listen, find common ground, and have a win-win.

Imagine If we could bring our networks together, first establishing their "why" and our common ground, then dream of the impact when a successful outcome materializes. If we could do this, we might even be able to provide global healthcare and the world with a better plan. It can all start with your network.

## 6. IF YOU ARE NOT HAVING FUN, YOU ARE DOING IT WRONG

I have a question for you — do not share the answer with anyone, this is just for self-reflection — when you leave a room or conversation, did you remove oxygen or add it? Is there more energy or is it depleted?

We all have moments of serious conversations that need to be serious, but for the other 98 percent of the time, are you that person who adds life, fun, energy, and oxygen to the situation? The answer is important for two reasons: one, this type of person builds a better, more effective network, and two, it could save lives — yours and others'. There is an abundance of research that supports this: The positivity and laughter that you deliver can change your life and that of those around you. Although this is well-researched, it has been poorly communicated to the general population.

### Laughter is the best medicine

On a final note, laughter is serious business. While humor hasn't traditionally had a natural home in the work environment, numerous studies along with lived experience have demonstrated both short- and long-term positive effects of integrating humour into networking. Humor and playful communication are also very effective in building a bedrock for a social relationship that can weather storms. The ability to inject humour not only creates positive feelings, it nurtures an emotional connection.[*]

Humour can take many different forms while still being work-appropriate. Integrating the opportunity for laughter into your life, whether it be in the form of watching a funny TV show for a few moments before bed or checking out memes over breakfast, is as important as daily stretching or eating a healthy diet. Those with a positive orientation towards humour find a renewed sense of energy by encouraging the intake of oxygen-rich air that stimulates your muscles and organs and increases endorphins circulating in the bloodstream. Humour provides the short-term benefits of stress relief and decreased tension, setting an individual up in the right state of mind for networking.

Laughter also has longer-term health benefits that improve an individual's quality of life, lightening their mental load and fighting off stress and even serious illnesses. Laughter and a positive state of mind cause the brain to trigger a chemical reaction to release neuropeptides capable of improving immunity. Natural endorphins that are released in response to laughter relieve aches and pains and make it easier to deal with the difficulties that arise in day-to-day life. In short, laughter can help lessen stress, depression, and anxiety, leading to individuals feeling happier and having higher self-esteem.

All of these benefits make the argument for the integration of humour and laughter into life; however, this isn't always a laughing matter. Some people may find it a difficult task to envision how to begin. It doesn't have to be hard. Start with a couple of items like a greeting card, a cartoon, or a photo in your workspace that makes

---

[*] Mayo Clinic Staff, "Stress relief from laughter? It's no joke," Mayo Clinic, Mayo Foundation for Medical Education and Research, September 22, 2023, https://www.mayoclinic.org /healthy-lifestyle/stress-management/in-depth/stress-relief/art-20044456.

you smile or feel positive. Finding humour in the challenging experiences of everyday life changes your outlook and encourages others to reframe their experiences in ways that build a sense of collegiality in the workplace. Humour may take time to develop, but each time you respond with a smile or chuckle as you look towards the future, you begin to build a healthier, more positive approach that will attract others to want to connect with you.

Go ahead and give it a try. Turn the corners of your mouth up into a smile and then give a laugh, even if it feels a little forced. Once you've had your chuckle, take stock of how you're feeling. Are your muscles a little less tense? Do you feel more relaxed or buoyant? That's the natural wonder of laughing at work.

Last homework assignment: Do a search on "social benefit of humour" and "health benefits of humour." Indulge yourself in both self-care and "giver" care for others — it is no laughing matter (see what I did there?). Hopefully, you laughed at my bad dad jokes.

## SUMMARY OF STEPHEN'S SIX-STEP METHODOLOGY TO NETWORKING

While this may be a non-linear journey following the steps that I have learned throughout my various careers, it is written with the intention to aid you in your creation of a network that is both effective and capable of producing a significant impact. I intentionally first introduced the work by Simon Sinek on the importance of knowing and communicating your "why," followed by Adam Grant's work on the impact of building a "giver" culture in your network. I then coupled those ideas with raising your consciousness of "quantity or quality" and identifying which works for your situation. My job, through providing the three examples of these in action, and displaying my personal vulnerability, was to show just how many times I have been wrong in my first judgment, which then delivered a wonderful surprise in return. I hope these examples were able to demonstrate the benefits and set the scene to explore your unique opportunity to build diverse teams into your network, ultimately bringing them together with an inclusive "why." In my experience, the icing on the cake that makes it all come together is to ensure that those in your network are having fun. I cannot emphasize enough that fun is the magical ingredient missing in teams and people's lives today.

Enjoy your journey! Smile and laugh! Be a giver!

**Stephen Brickell** is a value creation architect and former senior executive at IBM. He takes great pride in being titled *Not Normal* — especially by those who work with him. Employing value creation architecture in all that he does, he looks to challenge himself and others through divergent and differentiated thinking.

Stephen is currently the president and CEO of Fusion Universal Healthcare, where he is deploying his time and efforts to help reshape the way that rural healthcare is done, creating a system that is "built by clinicians to support clinicians," and ensuring that everyone can access the lifesaving healthcare they need, regardless of where they are located.

# THE POWER OF NETWORKING: A PERSONAL JOURNEY

### Murray Simser | Founder and CEO of CITIZN

**G**rowing up is pretty hard for all of us. I grew up in a time of neighbourhood bullies and a fear that the whole world was a mean place. I knew I would get beat up, humiliated, or worse still. My family faced challenges in the aftermath of the Second World War, which affected our unity and focus. But then we all have that kind of trouble, don't we? So, it was something of a surprise to this small kid from an insignificant neighbourhood in Toronto, the Beaches, that he succeeded beyond his wildest imaginings. I had quite an imagination — that is no small thing.

If you feel like you are too small to win, too weak to be powerful, too nervous to be respected, and too scared to believe, well, you too can win. I have felt all those things, yet here I stand, writing a story about my experiences to help the next generation.

If I could encapsulate the entire story in a single phrase, it would be that you must go to new places and try many new things until you find something that inspires you. That's it, it is that simple. This concept is the foundation of every story that includes a hero's journey. Make your life a quest and follow the hero's journey wherever it takes you, come what may!

I hope my story inspires you to believe in yourself and know that you are enough, you just have to put yourself out there.

## THE CALL TO ADVENTURE

My story starts the first year I attended university. I had travelled little, seen nothing, and knew nobody. So, I had zero chance of using my connections the way that the fancy kids did. I was surrounded by what seemed to me to be people more skilled, smarter, better connected, richer, and who seemed to be invited everywhere. It was so incredibly daunting and scary. I was a wreck of insecurity and did not really believe I had much to offer. But here I was at a major university in the nation's capital, Ottawa, a city of about a million people with the world at my feet — I just didn't know it yet.

I met tons of people in my first few months. Some invited me to attend events, some of which I liked and some I did not. The one I liked the most was an invitation to a political party meeting on campus. I knew *nothing* about it but went anyway. I met way more people outside of the university crowd who I would never have met had I said no to going to the meeting. This was the start of something magical.

Within a few years, I was working on Parliament Hill for a few members of Parliament and for a soon-to-be prime minister. I was twenty-one years old — mind blown. By thirty, Service Canada had purchased — and every Canadian had used — software from the company I founded. By forty-five I was building the future of our democracies: an AI, powered and owned by citizens, called DemocracyGPT with the support of many of the country's most influential people.

**Lesson:** It was not because I was special that I ended up with this; it was because I dared to try new things.

The Power of Networking: A Personal Journey | 127

## OVERCOMING FEARS AND INSECURITIES

I grew up working-class poor in a rough neighbourhood and in public housing. Not a promising start. I was the first member of my family to go to university. I felt insecure, lonely, and out of place. I was often bullied by my peers for being different and nerdy. I had few friends and no mentors. I felt like I did not belong anywhere.

Yet I kept doing one thing that, with hindsight, turned out to be the key to success — I kept believing that I was worthy. I kept putting myself out there, and I behaved nicely, politely, and dressed the part (suits). Guess what? That eventually led to my meeting many people who saw value in me. That was a wonderful feeling.

Remember, everyone has inherent value. When you are young you might think you have little to offer, but that is simply not true. Those in influential positions need help too! You might just have the right combination of characteristics to get them interested in what you can offer. Your unique personality and presence are all that is really required. When a successful person looks at you, they are looking for someone who is classy and bright. What is classy? It is an old-school way of describing someone who speaks with dignity and politeness, dresses properly for the function, and acts the part by not embarrassing themselves. That's it!

**Lesson:** Your unique value is inherent; believe in yourself and present your best self to the world.

## MEETING WITH THE MENTOR

I decided to go to an event after receiving some encouragement from my microeconomics professor, who became something of a mentor, or at least a guide who listened. My professor told me that networking was an essential skill for any ambitious young person, and that I had nothing to lose and everything to gain by attending the event. He also gave me some valuable tips:

1. Research the event and attendees beforehand
2. Prepare a brief, engaging introduction about yourself
3. Ask open-ended questions to start conversations
4. Listen actively and show genuine interest
5. Bring business cards and exchange with others
6. Follow up with new contacts within forty-eight hours

This advice may seem simple, but to a young, insecure person, it was a huge boost to my confidence. We often forget how big the world seems when we are young. The courage to try matters more than anything else.

**Lesson:** Seek guidance from those with experience and be open to learning practical skills that can boost your confidence.

## CROSSING THE THRESHOLD

When I arrived at Parliament Hill for a Liberal Party event, I felt overwhelmed by the grandeur and history of the place. I saw hundreds of people dressed in suits and ties, chatting and laughing with each other. I felt like an outsider, a stranger in a strange land. As I stood on the sidelines, I wondered if I would ever fit in. Then, out of the blue, someone asked who I was. From that point forward, the evening was a blur and one of the most exciting events I have ever attended. Everything was new. I ended up speaking with influential people and made contacts that would last a lifetime. I went home that night and began to believe that perhaps I could one day be just like them.

It turns out I did just that. These early introductions led directly to other introductions, that led to still more. Get it? Within a couple of years, I had met many influential people who would change my life and give me opportunities I never thought I would have.

> **Lesson:** Every new encounter is an opportunity. Be brave enough to step into unfamiliar territory, as it often leads to unexpected growth.

## FACING CHALLENGES

Throughout my life, I faced many tests, both from allies and adversaries, that might have made me run home and stop trying. Don't quit! Just as I had to overcome my shyness and approach people I did not know, the further along I went the more influential were the people I was meeting. This is both good and bad. Good because of the opportunities, bad because not everyone has your best interests at heart.

I often had to deal with rejection, not fitting in, and even threats from people less noble. When you combine your own imposter syndrome as a young person (this is natural, don't worry) with people who try to hurt you, it can be pretty devastating.

Don't quit when someone hurts you, or tries to. Pick yourself up and keep going. This is perhaps the hardest step of all — keeping faith when all seems dark and dangerous. We are built to retreat from things that hurt us. The best advice I can give you is this: Don't let anyone take away your dreams! You deserve success every bit as much as they do. You will sometimes lose, but when you do, don't lose the lesson.

I also encountered some friends who tried to discourage or sabotage me. These frenemies are everywhere. Be wary of easy offers, simple solutions, and shortcuts — there aren't any!

> **Lesson:** Resilience in the face of adversity is key. Learn from setbacks, and don't let fear of failure or rejection stop you from moving forward.

## THE ORDEAL

You will face many huge tests of character as you rise. There is no rise without being tested to your core. You will face pain! The pain's job is to test your resolve. Only the worthy shall pass. You are not expected to always win, but if you want to win you are expected to *never* quit. You must pick yourself up every time you fall down, until you succeed. That power is available to anyone, no matter how small or weak you feel you are. A winner is someone who never quits.

My own ordeals came during three phases of my life:

1.  Co-founding my first software company in California
2.  Becoming a public company CEO — twice
3.  Reimagining democracy to leave a legacy

As a twenty-something Gen-Xer, I co-founded a software company under the tutelage of two very powerful, well-known, and wealthy serial entrepreneurs. Why did they give me this shot? Because they knew me from my previous work with them. My employee performance impressed them enough to be invited to found a company with them. These fellow travellers gave me the confidence and support to learn how to do truly great things. The fact is that I didn't always do great — I often failed — but I never failed to learn the lesson when I lost.

Becoming a public company CEO when I had never done that before was nerve-wracking. The jump to CEO is perhaps a bigger and riskier jump than moving into management in the first place. The means to getting there is to have good relations with people because these jobs often go to people that are known to the investors. The more people you know, people who know what you do, the more likely you are to be invited to run a company as CEO. That's it. You don't apply for CEO jobs, you get invited. However, it's important to note that becoming a CEO might not be everyone's goal, and that's perfectly fine. This advice is applicable if leadership in business is your intention.

Now that I have succeeded, I've chosen to build something for posterity. That is to give something back to the society that built me. I call it CITIZN. Now, you would think it would be easy to do this after the long beginning to my career, but nothing could be further from the truth. Remember that once you climb a mountain, you'll generally see many more in front of you.

**Lesson:** Growth often comes through challenges. Embrace the tests that come your way, as they are shaping you for future success.

## THE REWARD

I did not realize the power of networking until much later in my life. I believe that most of my success is due to the network of people I developed. I owe much of my success to luck! Isn't that funny to consider? The truth is, we all owe much more to luck than to anything else.

Do you know how to maximize luck? Networking! The more people you meaningfully interact with, the better your odds of success. That luck plays such a huge role in our lives is a beautiful thing, I think. It is also something that should give you hope. You can influence your luck by controlling the quality and quantity of your networking.

You will be rewarded for networking when the universe conspires to get you the things you need to succeed. So, remember to put yourself out there and the universe will make it worth your while.

**Lesson:** Fate favours the bold!

## THE ROAD BACK

I am not sure exactly when it was that I was able to see clearly the power of networking or its impact on my life, but now I can. A few years ago, I began to speak at universities as both an adjunct and as a guest lecturer. These experiences brought me full circle.

To see the faces of these promising young students who have the world before them was to see myself for the very first time. I knew then what had happened in my life.

I mostly understood the beauty of my journey and learned the importance of having faith that in the end it will all work out. To make sure it does, build your network, no matter how small it is at the start.

## LESSONS SUMMARY

So, what is the lesson of this story? It is that networking is a powerful tool for young people who want to achieve their personal or professional goals. Networking can help you:

1. Access new opportunities, resources, and information
2. Gain valuable insights, perspectives, and feedback
3. Receive support, guidance, and mentorship
4. Develop your skills, confidence, and self-esteem
5. Expand your horizons, vision, and impact

But networking is not a magic bullet or a shortcut. It requires hard work, courage, persistence, and resilience. It also requires a willingness to step out of your comfort zone, face uncertainty, and embrace change.

So go ahead, young people. Go out your door. Step onto the road. Network with the world. You never know where you might be swept off to.

**Murray Simser** is a Silicon Valley serial tech entrepreneur and a political junkie whose software has been used by millions of people. He is the founder and CEO of CITIZN, an AI-powered platform that empowers citizens to shape their own democracy. CITIZN is built on societal networks, a revolutionary concept that Murray invented to create a more equitable and sustainable form of capitalism, without affecting investor returns. Murray has a track record of creating and scaling innovative software solutions that have reached every corner of the globe.

# TRANSITIONING

### Helen Hayward | Partner Emeritus, Western Management Consultants

## SHARED VALUES

David Tsubouchi and I share many valuable traits in common: being a visible minority in a competitive world, having to constantly prove ourselves, and the invaluable contribution we make to any environment to advance inclusion. Above all, we both enjoy meeting, engaging, learning, and growing new connections as we move through our journey in life. Over the years, we have stayed connected as we've evolved in our respective roles in the community and the working world.

I hope my story generates a smile on your face, or a nod or shake of your head at the opportunities and challenges that life throws at us. Most of us think about our journey through life in stages: early years of schooling, middle years of working, building a career, raising a family, and then the later years slowing down to post-work, when we contribute to the community and enjoy a slower pace of life from the fruits of our labour.

Here are my pay-it-forward insights to share with those of you who follow in our footsteps as you transition through your own stages in life.

## THE BEGINNING

I was born and raised in Hong Kong when it was still a British colony. I grew up in a Catholic girls' school in Hong Kong, wore uniforms, and had all-female classmates from kindergarten to Grade 13! I finished high school and immigrated as an international student to a university in Canada.

My journey of building my first network thus began when I started at McMaster University and lived in residence. As an eighteen-year-old away from home for the first time, I was at a loss, not academically but socially. I did not know how to dress or behave in a co-ed environment. My face turned red when a male classmate leaned over to talk to me in class! I spent many hours looking down at my shoes, tongue-tied.

I lucked out in getting to form fast friendships with a number of students who were in residence. They were curious about my cultural upbringing, and I needed support in navigating the complex world of co-education. My friends were fun, nonjudgmental, eager to help, generous with advice, and made me feel welcome. Besides, my clothes, shoes, and handbags were exotic compared to their jeans and T-shirts. They became my lifelong friends; we were support networks for each other in our careers, in life, in relationships, in raising families, in celebrations, and in coping with challenges. Without this invaluable network for life, I doubt I would be sitting here writing this chapter.

I learned that when I am open to new experiences and meeting new people, I expand my horizons and gain different perspectives. The term "networking" had not yet emerged in the vocabulary, so I was not conscientiously or methodically networking when I started working. On reflection, a number of those I networked with continued our relationships to this day on multiple fronts.

It is hard to distinguish networking from friendship. To me, one leads to another.

> **First insight to networking:** Start early, experiment, listen, learn, commit.

## THE MIDDLE – CAREER BUILDING

Like most baby boomers, we went to university and began working at various times. I did not have the luxury of bumming around Europe or travelling around the world for a year after graduation. I started working right away.

My career has had two distinct parts since joining the Canadian workforce after university.

The first half of my career was in the Ontario public service. I started as a land use planner and went on to finance director and chief administrative officer before finishing my public service career as CEO of two adjudicative tribunals. Across the span of about twenty-five years, I worked in a spectrum of sectors that ranged from economic development to transportation to public safety to justice. Along the way, I faced the highs and lows of navigating a work environment that had biases against women and visible minorities.

I had many lucky opportunities to advance and develop in different sectors and in different capacities. I was thriving and happy, until I got stuck at management level!

As an immigrant of Chinese descent, I grew up with family and cultural values of success that say "if you keep your head down and work hard, then you will be noticed." It took me a long time — and learning from a couple of missed career opportunities — to realize that it is not enough. I was frustrated and did not understand why recruitment decisions were made in favour of other candidates who seemed to be equally or less qualified. I ate some humble pie, did lots of self-reflection, and finally found the courage to seek advice about why I was not succeeding in getting ahead.

A wise person told me what I was missing: networking. If people do not know you, who you are and what your contributions can be, others will be way ahead of you. I learned then in mid-career the value and importance of networking to building a brand for yourself. When I started working, building my network was limited to my immediate work environment. So, the people in my network were those who already knew me. My eyes were opened to the need to transition and expand my horizons, and by extension, expand my network to a broader spectrum of people in different sectors, disciplines, and roles.

So, I had to learn first about what networking is all about and how to develop that new skill to enrich what I had proven I can do.

It is first about understanding yourself — your aspirations, your strengths, and your weaknesses. Know what you want and why. Then you can begin to find out who can enrich and help you, as well as open doors for you to get there. And yes, have many reflections and discussions with yourself and be true to yourself.

I reached out to people outside of my immediate circle to ask for honest feedback and suggestions for how I could improve my profile and practise my pitch and delivery. It's like a makeover! It did build confidence and enhanced my ability to speak comfortably about myself.

**Second insight:** Get out there and build your professional network! Learn from and adjust to feedback!

## THE LATE MIDDLE

After a very rewarding career in public service, I took a giant leap into the world of professional services. I transitioned into being a business consultant, advising the public and not-for-profit clients on how to solve business and organizational problems. I loved the work! But I did not know how to pivot to be an adviser versus a doer.

The lessons of the power of networking were different as I transitioned from one to the other. I had to learn, again, about building a different profile and how to reshape and expand my networks. This was a lot tougher than I'd thought. How to reinvent oneself in mid- to late career is humbling and scary! I needed courage but also sound advice and help.

Once again, I dove into my Rolodex and began to reflect on who could advise me with generosity, wisdom, and no judgment. Many before me had entered the profession of consultants — lots to learn.

I had to learn and develop new relationships with former colleagues whom I worked well with together as peers. Flipping the relationship requires a reframing and rebuilding of those relationships. I had to do this one by one.

One of my reliable network friends, who had made the leap into the world of technology consulting before me, said to me: "Your network is only relevant for two years. People you know will be obsolete because they move around every two to three years. You have to keep up with constant networking to keep the relationships current and up to date." To me that advice was like a mantra at the back of my head even to this day. Trying to keep up with people's movement is a full-time job!

I found using LinkedIn very helpful for business purposes. You have the choice of selecting and sharing information with those you wish to include in your networks. I was able to build a successful and rewarding consulting, coaching, and executive search practice that spanned twenty years with a little bit of help from my friends. Some of my long-time clients remain on my active network. There is great comfort in knowing there are people you can rely on and talk to who are just a call, email, or text away!

140 | The Ripple Effect

> **Third insight:** At this stage of your career, be smart and strategic about networking. But above all, keep it up and keep it current!

## THE MATURE STAGE

Many of us have found that after building a life of success in careers and rewarding work, it is time to give back. I chose to give back by volunteering to serve on boards whose missions aligned with my values and beliefs: healthcare, higher education, social justice, and equity.

But where do you begin? How do you find the right opportunity that matches your interests and capabilities? Every day, I hear from my networks, mostly women and visible minorities, that the world of boards, both non-profit and for-profit, is a big secret. It seems like people get the prized opportunity because of who they know, and it was back to square one with the workplace biases from my early career. Things come full circle!

I see myself as a community builder and generously serve on not-for-profit and public boards. One of the most memorable and valuable experiences for me was joining a professional corporate planning association called the Planning Executives Institute (PEI). The membership was made up of professional planners in business and public sectors in financial services, investment, real estate, and auto industries across Canada. I volunteered my time and effort to serve on the executive of the Toronto chapter of PEI, eventually becoming the chapter president. It was exhilarating and intimidating at times for me to rub shoulders with senior planning executives from Magna, Ernst & Young, BMO, etc. Many of them were more senior, experienced, older, and wiser than I was. I was also a lone woman in a predominantly male world! I pushed myself hard to network with

Transitioning | 141

each of them and to develop trusting relationships with the chapter board and membership of five hundred.

I knew I had succeeded when I was elected president of the Toronto chapter and guided it to becoming the largest chapter in North America, surpassing New York! If I had not done the homework and legwork on networking with my peers, I don't think I would have been successful. For that effort and support of my peers, I received a Lifetime Achievement Award from the organization.

I had to overcome the challenges to my self-confidence, push myself out of my comfort zone, reach out to people I normally would not have considered, and establish a culture and practice with my peers. So, thank you Alan, Charlie, Tim, Rick, Jeff, and others who became my staunch network of corporate supporters!

## OPENING DOORS

One of my most rewarding relationships came when someone I knew and worked well with as a peer called me unexpectedly. Jean was chairing the governance committee and leading board recruitment for Seneca College of Applied Arts and Technology in the Toronto area. She reached out to me and asked if I would be interested in joining the board. Yes, I was. It was the right time and the right opportunity. That was where I renewed acquaintance with David and other business and community leaders who were stellar board members at that time. I subsequently succeeded Jean as board chair.

Fast forward a few years to when the college president happened to chair the governance committee of Sunnybrook Health Sciences, a world-renowned academic health sciences centre in Toronto, and recruited me to join the hospital board. I served for nine years on the Sunnybrook board and networked with CEOs and senior executives of global business, banks, real estate, and the healthcare industry. Serving on a world-class hospital board is at the top for not-for-profit importance and prestige. My board peers expanded my network to a global stage and into different business sectors that I otherwise might not have been exposed to.

The hospital board experience led me to join the board of the Ontario Hospital Association, which represents 140-plus hospitals in Ontario as the collective voice of hospital care. My network has since multiplied to include hospital CEOs and trustees from all corners of the province. This giving and receiving of community service and personal development was beyond my wildest expectations.

That higher education board experience led me to join bigger boards in the healthcare, justice, and immigration sectors at provincial, national, and international levels. All these subsequent opportunities were from one network peer to another, to another and another, as my governance competency, community-building interest, and reputation grew.

As a governor, trustee, or independent board member, I have met and enriched my life with a wide range of leaders in business, government, and community in Canada and around the world. My fellow board members come from depths of experiences in executive management, political leadership, and community building and a breadth of expertise, knowledge, and skills.

One question I am constantly asked is, how do I get on a board? The short answer is: Start networking! Let people know what you are looking for and how you can contribute. Expanding to that "outer ring" of your network requires careful thought and strategic focus.

To this day, I am grateful for the initial door-opener twenty-plus years ago. I have since followed that example by conscientiously and strategically reaching out to my networks and thoughtfully broadening my relationships to those outside of my comfort zone.

**Fourth insight:** Get involved in community building – it broadens your networks and horizons.

## TOOLKIT FOR NETWORKING

Networking takes time and energy. Not every network opportunity is helpful. Here are some of the tools I used to sustain my continuous networking.

Many people who work are very mobile and move around in their career, in their roles, in different departments, different organizations, different sectors. I made it a practice to keep up to date on their career movement and contact information. I also became a contact source for my consulting colleagues at work. My Rolodex was a constant work of art!

I stay in contact with select people in my networks: I pick up the phone or send an email to say hello and catch up. People like to be contacted, to feel valued or cared about. When possible, I arrange to meet for cappuccinos to keep the personal relationship warm. I have many cappuccino meet-ups, and I got to know all the best cafés in downtown Toronto that are quiet and offer some privacy.

I do look for one to two events each year that cover emerging topics of interest with interesting speakers, and with potential participants who are not in my immediate circle. I often come away having widened my circle with new and different additions to my evolving network.

## KNOW YOURSELF

So often in my consulting, coaching, and mentoring practice, the person in front of me could not articulate what they want or need. I found it impossible to help them, to know who in my network I could introduce them to. The "how" can only follow if "what" and "why" are there to guide your journey. So be prepared before you begin the conversation.

## PAY IT FORWARD

As everyone will tell you, networking is a two-way street. As much as you ask, you also give. As I engage with those who follow me, I encourage them to think outside of their network, reach out or ask to be introduced to someone they don't know but may be able to help, advise, or open doors for. It takes courage, planning ahead, and humility when barriers are in the way.

Networking is a lifelong journey, not a sprint. It's important to give as much as you receive, and just as rewarding. The shy, tongue-tied foreign student you met at the beginning of this chapter is now a confident, outgoing, actively engaged citizen, thriving in volunteer board, social, and family networks!

Keep building, keep expanding. I am.

Enjoy your journey. It will be worth it.

**Helen Hayward** is a dedicated community builder who advocates for positive change, removes systemic barriers, and collaborates with leaders and partners to learn and to contribute. She is an experienced independent board director of numerous international, federal, provincial, and not-for-profit boards in the health, justice, and higher education sectors.

Prior to consulting, she had a successful career in the provincial government of Ontario, beginning as a transportation planner, to CFO and CIO of justice ministries, to assistant attorney general, and finishing as CEO of two land-use adjudicative tribunals.

Personally, Helen actively mentors young professionals and is a wellness practitioner and loving GG (glamorous grandmother).

# THE POWER OF FRIENDSHIP THROUGH CULTURE

### Chris Hope | Lawyer and President of the Japanese Canadian Cultural Centre

In any conversation about networking, you'll find many references to developing meaningful, collaborative relationships, authenticity, fulfillment, generosity, and gratitude. Each of those elements is critical to the art, but I'd like to add another dimension to the discussion: survival.

I am a Yonsei, a fourth-generation Japanese Canadian, born and raised in Toronto. I'm a lawyer by trade, but I've temporarily put my legal practice on hold to focus full-time on serving as the volunteer president of the Japanese Canadian Cultural Centre.

I fit the mold of a corporate networker. I recently delivered the keynote address at the national conference of the Federation of Asian Canadian Lawyers on the power of taking control of narratives. In the past couple of months, I've boarded planes with big ideas, limited contacts, and tentative plans, but have been able to move past gatekeepers to quickly form what I hope will become meaningful relationships with some exceptional people that many would have considered completely inaccessible.

The magic ingredient for me? I never feel like I'm alone. My work is part of a grand continuum that was established to benefit not only all Canadians but people around the globe who are willing to put aside differences, to build bonds of *friendship through culture*. That's where the element of survival comes into the mix.

David Tsubouchi noted how his experience of growing up as a Sansei, that is, a third-generation Japanese Canadian, shaped his development from a naturally shy person to the realization that he had the power to effect change, to speak up, and to break through barriers in society. For a member of the Japanese Canadian community in Toronto, that was not only a significant personal achievement, but also one the entire community could be proud of after generations of perseverance, hard work, and sacrifice *just to have a voice*.

———

During the Second World War, all Canadians of Japanese ancestry were stripped of their rights of citizenship, based purely upon their race. Their property was confiscated, never to be returned, and they were incarcerated.

My mother, a third-generation Canadian, was among them. At 2½ years old, her citizenship was stripped, and she was declared to be an "enemy alien." My grandparents were separated and incarcerated, and my grandfather was then sent to a government labour camp in the interior of British Columbia and Alberta.

Prior to the war, approximately 99 percent of the Japanese Canadian community lived west of the Rocky Mountains. When the war ended in 1945, Japanese Canadians were forcibly dispersed east of the Rockies, forbidden by the government from returning west until 1949, with no justification other than racist politics.

No treasonous act was ever recorded among the Japanese Canadian population, despite the many efforts at the time to vilify them. On the contrary, the population was noted as being exemplary in following government directions as they were systematically stripped of everything they had.

There was one lesson that many members of the Japanese Canadian population took to heart over the course of their struggles in Canada before, during, and — as they continued to face racism and prejudice — after the War.

Hatred is fuelled by racism, division, and prejudice. But there is one simple antidote that can overcome all: friendship.

———

Fast forward to 1964 in Toronto. With great community fanfare, the Japanese Canadian Cultural Centre was officially opened in June. Prime Minister Lester B. Pearson stood on the front steps of the brand new JCCC and stated:

> For me, this centre is a reminder of the multi-racial heritage on which our nation is being built, surely and strongly. It is a new living monument to the fact that our Canadian purpose which seeks a Canadian identity, need not and does not mean a loss of the traditions and cultures, the arts and skills brought to Canada from other lands . . . I hope that the Centre will serve as a reminder to future generations of Japanese Canadians that theirs is an abundant heritage and a proud tradition.[*]

Prime Minister Pearson's speech not only marked a significant change in the government's view of the contributions of the Japanese Canadian community to the fabric of Canadian society, but it stands as the first public articulation of the concept of multiculturalism, which continues as the official policy of Canada to this day.

That breakthrough is a shining example of the power of effective networking. The story of how it happened is a source of daily inspiration for me.

---

[*] Lester B. Pearson, Official Opening Ceremony of the Japanese Canadian Cultural Centre, June 7, 1964.

The JCCC was established by seventy-five families that mortgaged their own homes to guarantee the construction loan to build it. Nearly every one of those families had been left destitute by the Canadian government just twenty years earlier. The JCCC was opened with the motto "Friendship through culture."

The simple idea was to open a gathering place to *all* Canadians to share a common interest in aspects of Japanese culture. From martial arts to flower arrangements to cooking, bonds of friendship would be formed among participants in activities from all backgrounds. Those bonds would then break down any of the perceived barriers of otherness that could otherwise be exploited to tear Japanese Canadians out of the fabric of Canadian society — again.

The stories of the individuals in the community, willing to put everything on the line to work together to support their deep belief in the deceptively simple founding concept of friendship through culture — to make the country a better place — sent a message that could not be ignored. The prime minister and his cabinet empathized with the messengers, and a new national policy was formed.

Seemingly overnight, a group of marginalized Canadians that had continuously fought prejudice for two generations were recognized as model citizens. Eventually, all Canadians would have the legal and policy tools that are still relied upon to make it clear that prejudice is no longer tolerated at any level in Canadian society. Though the reality remains that true equality will always be a work in progress.

Here we are, sixty years later. The majority of the membership of the JCCC has now shifted to Canadians with no Japanese ancestry. In a geopolitical climate where the words "war" and "genocide" sadly dominate the news cycle, the lessons of friendship through culture have never been more critical, and the JCCC stands as a model cultural centre for the world.

In spite of total disenfranchisement and what must have seemed like insurmountable obstacles of prejudice, the founders of the JCCC built a broad network of supporters that have continued to lift the organization and share the spirit of friendship through culture to this day.

But, after multiple generations of development and expansion, the JCCC is running at capacity. Its traditional base of support is diminishing and needs to be augmented urgently, with new sources of financing, support, and partnership. A generational change is taking place among the leadership of the organization, and the challenge is to keep the organization just as vibrant and effective — even more so — for at least another sixty years.

Networking for the JCCC is once again mission critical. As president, I'm in the driver's seat, and I am grateful to have a lifetime of networking experience to call upon to drive this new mission forward. My networking "toolkit" is a top ten list that I reflect upon every day in the course of my own networking journey.

## TIP #10: KNOW WHO YOU ARE BEFORE YOU WALK INTO THE ROOM

"In the legal profession, there are finders, minders, and grinders. Figure out what you are early, and it will make your life a lot easier." That's what my Bay Street law firm mentor told me at our first meeting,* and it's an important lesson that has stuck with me ever since.

In the law firm business, finders are charismatic hustlers that bring new business to a firm. Minders maintain that business, balancing client relations and a high degree of professional skill. Grinders rank highest on the professional skill side of things, but in many cases are seen to lack the emotional intelligence to represent the best face of the business to clients.

The simple message is to honestly identify and play to your strengths. Feedback from those around you will be key, whether among existing mentors or from members of entirely new audiences. All you have to do is ask.

The other important lesson here is that people you interact with constantly form judgments, and they will quickly lump you into a

---

\* Larry Weinberg, Cassels Brock and Blackwell LLP — thanks, Larry.

The Power of Friendship Through Culture | 151

category similar to those mentioned above. Aligning your self-awareness with the image you *actually* project can supercharge your effectiveness in building relationships.

### TIP #9: PROMOTE MUTUAL BENEFITS

"How can I help you?" That's the question I carefully consider prior to any networking interaction. You can get to the answer a million different ways, but leading with a genuine and mutually aligned proposition is the ideal one for constructively proceeding towards an eventual ask.

Genuine relationship building isn't built on quid pro quo, it's pulling together in the same direction for a bigger purpose.

### TIP #8: NEVER LOOK DOWN

Take risks. Every interaction brings with it the possibility of rejection. You need to have a thick skin. Shikata ga nai, as my grandmother taught me: "It can't be helped." You can only control what you can control. It's pointless wasting your energy on worrying about anything else.

### TIP #7: BELIEVE, BELIEVE, BELIEVE

If you don't believe in what you're selling, you're never going to convince anyone of anything. By the time I go into a meeting, in an ideal world and with a proper amount of prep time, I am so excited about the ideas that I hope to communicate that I need to pause before I speak to contain my enthusiasm. I'm not entering a room to "sell," I'm entering a room to recruit evangelists to a cause. People pick up on that, and genuine enthusiasm is contagious.

## TIP #6: NARRATIVE IS YOUR BEST FRIEND

Telling stories is one of the most powerful things humans can do to inspire, influence, and teach. Refine the stories that you hope to share in advance. You may not even get the chance to tell them. But if you do, they should be on point, to the point, and have a beginning, middle, and end.

## TIP #5: COMMON INTERESTS ARE ACCELERANTS

Passion is an incredibly powerful connector. Music and an appreciation for mechanical engineering are two of my passions. I'm not very good at either but am endlessly fascinated by conversations about Led Zeppelin bootlegs, old sports cars, and tools and carpentry. Shared interests are like memberships in the same club. They're a shortcut to familiarity.

Shared experiences fall into this category as well. Golf doesn't particularly excite me, but its utility as a connector is obvious.

## TIP #4: BE GRATEFUL

Never take your ability to gain access to new networking opportunities for granted. Networking is a privilege, and doors are seldom opened without help. Make sure to properly express and follow up with gratitude after every opportunity that your contacts have assisted you with, particularly those that have taken risks to do so on your behalf. Your referrers deserve credit for every win.

## TIP #3: AUTHENTICITY IS CREDIBILITY

The faster you can communicate why you're personally invested in the reason that you're seeking a connection, the more authenticity you have as the right person for the conversation. Coming across as disingenuous is fatal to successful networking.

"Skin in the Game" is the theme song of a music documentary called *The Immediate Family* that was recently released. The lyrics jumped out at me as really driving the "authenticity" concept home in a networking context:

*You've got to stand close to the flame.*
*You've got to have skin in the game.*
*You've got to have heart in your game.*
*You've got to have soul in your game.*
*You've got to have pride in your game.*
*You've got to have skin in the game.*
*It's more than the money,*
*It's more than the fame.*
*It's about giving your all,*
*It's about skin in the game.*[*]

## TIP #2: CULTURE EATS EVERYTHING FOR BREAKFAST

Do your homework regarding the cultural context for your interactions. That includes aspects of corporate and political culture, but also national culture. If, for instance, you expect to form a bond and close a deal with a brand-new Japanese business contact over the course of a weekend — forget it!

Business relationships need time and attention to develop in Japan. Japan is a collectivist society where business success is measured over decades, and corporate success is seen in the context of benefits to the company and to society at large, over time. A far cry from the Western expectation of driving success on a quarterly basis.

---

[*] The Immediate Family, "Skin in the Game," track 9 on *Skin in the Game*, Quarto Valley, February 16, 2024. Lyrics reproduced with permission.

Personal trust is critical before business is even discussed, and that can generally only be achieved by spending time together over multiple meetings. You need to prepare yourself for a lot of silence in the course of those conversations as well. While you may feel at an awkward loss for words at times, your contact may be perceiving you as being wise for taking a pause in the conversation. Again, quite counterintuitive for Westerners.

## TIP #1: MIND YOUR MANNERS

Business etiquette training is the place to start for intercultural networking. Manners will communicate far more than language when you're forming critical first impressions.

Mom was right all along.

**Chris Hope** has been the president of the Japanese Canadian Cultural Centre since 2022, guiding the sixty-year-old organization — the largest Japanese cultural centre in the world outside of Japan — through a period of strategic and structural change. In 2011, he co-founded the Toronto Japanese Film Festival (TJFF) at the JCCC. For most of its existence, the TJFF has maintained its status as the highest-grossing Japanese language film festival in the world outside of Japan. As a corporate and entertainment lawyer and chartered corporate director, Chris Hope has received multiple awards for his legal work and advocacy. He is a passionate community builder.

# THE POWER OF MEANINGFUL NETWORKING

### Anna Paluzzi | Former Senior Adviser to Metrolinx CIO

My parents, both born in a small village in the Apennine Mountains of Italy, immigrated to Canada in the early '50s, settling in Sault Ste. Marie, Ontario. My father, Gino, a skilled tailor trained in Rome, aspired to establish his own successful tailoring business once he was settled in Canada. After studying, learning the English language, and saving enough money, he opened Gino's Tailor Shop, affectionately known as The Shop.

The Shop, located in our renovated home, became my haven. Little did I know, at that young age, that I was already immersed in the art of networking. Growing up with a work-at-home dad in the '60s, I now recognize his conscious and caring approach to networking as his superpower.

Spending countless hours in The Shop, I observed my dad at work, interacting with customers and sewing away. The bancone, a large structure serving as a workspace and reception area, illustrates a crucial lesson. My dad would always come around to the front of the bancone to enthusiastically greet each person who entered. The lesson? To make oneself approachable, we must remove the physical and emotional barriers. Authenticity, open body language, and a genuine care for others are the keys to fostering connections. This power to connect not only shaped my childhood but also opened the door to my very first job.

One of my dad's cherished customers, the director of the Sault Ste. Marie Public Library, played a pivotal role in my career. During their conversations, my dad would inquire about job opportunities for me. Thanks to his exemplary relationship-building skills, this connection allowed me to step into the workforce. What an amazing and fulfilling experience this was for me to learn how to connect and build relationships with my colleagues and the patrons of the library.

## NEXT STOP: THE BIG CITY AND BIG CHALLENGES

Encouraged by my father to "do more with my life," I pursued higher education at the University of Toronto, drawn to the vibrant city where my brother had settled. Networking became crucial as I sought out a job at the Metropolitan Toronto Public Library. By leveraging my dad's principles, I secured a part-time position while pursuing my studies. Starting over in a large city was exciting but also daunting for a small-town young woman.

In the '90s, social media and online platforms were nonexistent, and the way I immersed myself in the emerging culture was by building relationships with others. Some found my small-town and often naïve mindset endearing, while others did not share the same sentiment. Being genuine and respectful in your interactions with others generally makes people more open, but it's important to remember there is no one-size-fits-all approach to relationship building. I faced challenges, but I aimed to learn from the experience each time without being too hard on myself. Embracing both positive and negative networking experiences is inevitable; however, the most valuable lesson was learning from my mistakes. It underscored the point that not everyone has to fit into your circle or network.

The "work" in network is intentional. Leaving the familiar confines of my hometown for Toronto was a transformative yet overwhelming experience. Establishing connections and making friends was challenging in a larger city. Building a network from scratch required genuine respect for diverse backgrounds and a willingness to learn from our differences. In this part of my journey, I made a lot of incredible connections and found that I was drawn to people with whom I shared common values.

## THE WORK IN NETWORKING

The importance of networking became even clearer in my professional life. A quote by business networking expert Ivan Misner encapsulates it well: "You have to get out there and connect with people. It's not called net-sitting or net-eating. It's called networking. You have to work at it."[*]

Networking isn't a one-and-done endeavour. It takes effort to nurture and strengthen your relationships. Over two decades later, the lessons remain as important as ever. While technology has introduced various avenues for networking, the emphasis on quality over quantity endures. Nurturing relationships is essential to unlocking the true power of networking. The goal is not merely collecting contacts but transforming connections into meaningful, long-lasting relationships.

Leadership and networking are interconnected concepts. I had the privilege of meeting Jim Collins, the author of *Good to Great*, at a conference. When questioned about the traits of great leaders, he underscored humility as a pivotal quality. No single individual possesses all the skills, talents, and knowledge in the world. Understanding this, exceptional leaders surround themselves with individuals who bring diverse strengths to the table, fostering a robust team. This philosophy is equally applicable to networking — surround yourself with a variety of individuals or groups who encompass strengths and skills that complement your own. A diversity of skills and perspectives amplifies the collective power of your network.

---

[*] Ivan Misner, "It's Not Net-Sit or Net-Eat — It's Called Network," July 2, 2018, https://ivanmisner.com/its-not-net-sit-or-net-eat-its-called-network/. Dr. Misner founded Business Network International in 1985 and is the author of *Networking Like a Pro* (2009).

## NETWORKING TO HELP OTHERS SUCCEED

As I reflect on my career, sharing knowledge and helping others to succeed truly fulfills me. Watching my colleagues grow and succeed and knowing that I played a part in that is one of the greatest gifts. I would go so far as to say that this is my superpower and the part of my career that I am most proud of.

Establishing "Communities of Practice" centred on new grads and young professionals allowed me to contribute to their immediate network. By bringing them into my network and facilitating interactions with colleagues, customers, and partners, I strengthened the concept of networking. Leading by example holds significant power, as team members closely observe their leaders, so it can reinforce the value of networking and help members of your team build this skill along the way. Demonstrating approachability, a willingness to share experiences, and making an effort to know people are some of the greatest things you can pass on to them. It's important to remember that networking isn't solely a top-down activity. Create space for reverse mentoring and learn from them as well — it is amazing what they can teach you!

Be generous with your network. Don't just try to build a relationship when you need something from someone. Make time for others. Part of being genuine and authentic means that you give selflessly and support others without expecting anything in return. Give the gift of your connections to help others in times of need. My own success would not have been possible without the incredible individuals in my network who took the time and made the effort to introduce me to people. The true potential of your network grows exponentially when shared with others.

## AUTHENTICITY IS *KEY*

In the age of AI, technology can aid learning and growth, but essential human traits — empathy, authenticity, and relationship building — remain irreplaceable.

Networking is a skill that is accessible to everyone, capable of being learned and cultivated. It's an adventure that opens doors to unexpected opportunities. If the idea of networking seems daunting, start by prioritizing active listening. Understanding others is a remarkable way to initiate connections. When people sense they are being heard, it often encourages them to open up and form a connection with you. Observe individuals who excel at networking and let trusted connections serve as guides in your own networking journey.

Walk the talk. Drawing inspiration from role models, mentors, and coaches, I believe in the gradual and purposeful building of connections. Be open to serendipitous moments, as you can often build connections in the most unexpected places. Every interaction presents an opportunity to network, whether it's the person sitting next to you on an airplane, someone alone in the lunchroom, or the individual in line at the coffee shop. A simple smile or greeting can initiate a conversation that might lead to unexpected connections. Don't overlook these simple opportunities to connect with others; they can be valuable in fostering meaningful relationships.

———

I started this chapter by talking about my childhood and now I have reached the end of my working days, or as I like to call it, my "rewirement." I continue to keep my network alive and growing through volunteering, my travels, and in my everyday life, but most importantly, my network helps others now more than ever. As I reflect on my life and journey, I realize the most important accomplishments and greatest joys aren't about anything tangible. They are about the relationships I've forged throughout all stages of my life, the people whose lives I've positively impacted and those who have had the most profound impact on me.

**Anna Paluzzi** is the former senior adviser to Metrolinx's chief information officer, where she played a pivotal role in their digital transformation. Previous to Metrolinx, she held several positions at Canadian Tire throughout their digital transformation, including chief of staff to the chief technology officer, leader of a community of practice for citizen developers, and digital portfolio manager. Building a career in the world of change management, communication, and technology, her extensive and varied career has spanned healthcare, education, retail, telecom, and transportation. This has not only equipped her with a wealth of knowledge and experience but has also fostered a deep love for technology.

Recently embracing the next chapter of semi-retirement or, as she affectionately refers to it, "rewirement," Anna has transitioned into the role of an independent consultant, where her passion for driving organizational success through digital transformation continues to thrive.

# THE ENTREPRENEURIAL JOURNEY: FROM NFQ TO NETWORKING

### Yung Wu | Serial Entrepreneur and Former CEO, MaRS Discovery District

When David Tsubouchi first asked me to write a chapter for his new book on networking, I was flattered — and then struggled with writer's block as I stared at the flashing cursor on a blank screen, wondering what I had signed myself up for. After all, as a lifelong serial (most would say compulsive) entrepreneur, I have made my way by blazing new trails that did not rely upon conventional wisdom from others, pushing through objections and inventing new futures that I envisioned but others did not yet see. And to top things off, I'm a self-declared introvert who is terrible at small talk — I'm actually not interested in weather updates as conversation starters, and I'm not a social drinker!

What the heck would I know about "networking," and why had I agreed to do this anyways?

And then it dawned on me — it was David who had asked. David and I are fellow directors and friends on the board of one of Canada's great pension plans, and we have developed a relationship of immense respect and appreciation. And that was it — as soon as I reframed "acquiring casual networks" into "developing meaningful relationships," everything fell into place. Genuine relationships are earned — not granted. And while we never "keep track" in a ledger, the gives and takes tend to balance out in a fair exchange over the course of years and decades, if one is lucky.

Entrepreneurs navigate tremendous headwinds and perfect storms to invent their futures. But deep relationships with a few very special guides — honed through significant outside challenges — are the key to the resilience and wisdom that is required to map the trail and to survive and thrive in the journey ahead.

But let me not get ahead of myself — I'd like to first share a bit about my own journey as an entrepreneur to provide context for my reflections.

## OPENING THOUGHTS

Why is it that, in most cases, entrepreneurs who start companies rarely make the transformation into becoming the CEOs who grow the enterprises to critical mass? Or that so many start-ups fail after tremendous initial growth and promise?

After going through several tours of duty as an entrepreneur and business founder, before moving into CEO and chairman roles in growing, complex, venture-backed enterprises, and then finally joining the "dark side" by becoming a private equity investor myself, it has become clear to me that it takes very different competencies and guiding principles to succeed at each stage. What is common sense and self-evident at each stage could be poison to the next (and vice versa). These transition points represent significant risks for stakeholders (including original founders) unless there is a strong commitment to making the necessary personal adjustments and changes so that the organization is enabled and empowered to realize its potential at all times.

# NFQ

I have an enormous amount of respect for my fellow entrepreneurs. After building and achieving liquidity events for five of my own companies, I decided that it was time to give back to the next generation of entrepreneurs. That's when I decided to start my own family office venture capital platform, NFQ Ventures. NFQ comes from "never f***ing quit," and it's one of the core values embedded into every one of the companies that I have built and led. I don't think it should be easy to "fail fast." Pivot fast, learn fast, adapt fast — but it should never be easy to quit fast.

I founded my first company more than two decades ago on a couple of credit cards and a dream. After two major market cycles, three major rounds of financing, three business model changes, and two economic perfect storms, I reached the conclusion that success and failure are simply different points along the same continuum and that every human being and business will eventually encounter both. Probably many times.

Getting through all these cycles wasn't just about foresight, strategic vision, competitive strategy, customer relationship management, innovation, time to market, or any of a number of factors that most business pundits focus on. Yes, all these factors are important, but the one consistent ingredient required to survive and thrive is resilience — the determination to face each and every challenge with an act of will and to rapidly adapt to anything that is thrown at us.

An apocryphal quote often attributed to Winston Churchill probably said it best: "Success is not final; failure is not fatal. It is the courage to continue that counts."

Look, everyone will applaud, remark upon, and celebrate your brilliance when things are going your way. But I propose that you are defined by how you react when times are tough, when you don't have momentum on your side, and when you wake up to a daily, weekly, monthly diet of adversity. Do you exhibit grace under fire? What does your leadership look like when things aren't going your way? Do your people continue to follow you when you must climb uphill? What about when the bullets start flying? Are you able to take decisive, tough actions while continuing to hold the hearts and minds of your team? How do you keep all your stakeholders informed and aligned to a common purpose when all the external forces are working to splinter your coalition?

———

The single biggest challenge for my first company occurred shortly after we raised our third and last major round of financing in June 2001 — the single largest private financing round for the tech sector in Canada, even after the collapse of the tech space in the dot-com tech bust. At the time, we had almost four hundred employees, were growing annually by 50 percent, and were six months away from an initial public offering (IPO). A few months later, 9/11 hit our customers hard, only to domino into the market failures of Tyco, Enron, Anderson, and eventually AIG and Lehman Brothers as the Great Recession of 2008 took shape. The entire North American general insurance sector (our primary customer base) went into a tailspin — the worst time in its history.

Major tech investment programs were the first initiatives to get cut by our customers and prospects, as everyone began conserving cash and reducing discretionary expenditures. We went from a market where we were winning 60 percent of the available deals to having no deal flow available for the next twenty-four months. Instead of preparing for an IPO, we ended up facing a sudden and catastrophic downturn in our business.

Bad markets trump good management and great products. So, we took immediate action to conserve cash, restructure the company, and hunker down to ride out the cycle and survive nuclear winter in our space. We undertook the toughest and most painful actions of my entire entrepreneurial career, exiting every major long-term obligation, shutting down all non-core operations, slashing expenses down to "life support," and dismantling much of the company that I had carefully built up over twelve years.

## TRUSTED RELATIONSHIPS ARE EARNED, NOT GRANTED

That should have been the end of my story — but it was not. We were able to lean on deep, high-quality relationships with key employees, customers, partners, investors, advisers, and backers, relationships we had invested in throughout our entire entrepreneurial journey. And they were the source of our resilience when it came time to navigate the most challenging of times for the industry in two decades. To this day, I fervently believe that great, lasting relationships are forged and strengthened through challenge. They are earned and tested over time, and hard-won trust is the real return when it comes to colleagues and stakeholders who will have your back during times of challenge — not just when things are going well.

In spite of all the pain that shareholders, customers, employees, and founders collectively shared, my leadership team and I received complete and continued backing through all of these tough actions. We outlasted the market cycle with our intellectual property (IP) and a small core team intact. We rebuilt the company with substantially the same top-notch employees we had been forced to release during the downturn. The tough actions we took resulted in a very lean, efficient operating model and a vastly simplified equity structure and balance sheet. This allowed us to reposition the team and the IP for global leadership in our space, eventually leading to a very successful billion-dollar liquidity event with one of the world's largest enterprise software companies.

The bottom line is that you must bring aspiration, inspiration, and velocity during times of growth while being prepared to pivot drastically to the conservation of scarce resources and stockpiling choices at times of tremendous challenge. At all times, one must stay committed to delivering on promises made, being decisive and action-oriented, and honouring obligations to stakeholders over the long term.

———

The keys to sustainable, successful business performance are a determination to never quit, an ability to constantly adapt, and receiving the continued backing and support of your most critical stakeholders. Having the tenacity to keep going is the one thing that is within our ability to decide. And if you have the trusted relationships to sustain and support you, you give yourself the opportunity to choose the nature and timing of the "Kodak moments" within the continuum that determine your own so-called overnight successes.

So, let's return to the imperative of developing trusted, meaningful relationships in an entrepreneurial journey. Over decades of building companies and leading organizations that are global in scope, I have gotten to know and do business with many people. But it takes time to earn authentic two-way trust. Trust can be the strongest fabric that binds relationships together. And yet, that fabric is woven from the most fragile threads.

It turns out that a few deeply personal, trusted relationships have always been at the heart of my ability to survive and thrive through the inevitable challenges that come in life as an entrepreneur.

## PARALLEL TRACKS: IMMIGRANT EXPERIENCES AND THE ENTREPRENEURIAL JOURNEY

My journey from an immigrant to a serial entrepreneur mirrors the entrepreneurial path itself — it was fraught with challenges, marked by adaptability, and rich in lessons. As immigrants, we started with nothing except for our own capabilities, fierce determination, and a deeply held sense of gratitude to our adopted country.

I remember landing with my mother and sister in Ville d'Anjou, Montreal, in the 1960s, in an English block of a French borough of the city. We might have been the first visible minority ever seen by the locals — quickly becoming a circus sideshow that others gawked and made jokes at when they saw us on the street. I did not speak English or French at the time, and I don't know who was more shocked — us or the local residents. After all, they had never seen an Asian in person before, just as I had never been called a "Chink" until then. Asian people were stereotyped into caricatures like Hop Sing — an obsequious manservant with buck teeth and a pigtail in a popular TV show called *Bonanza*; or the evil Fu Manchu, an oriental supervillain who was the epitome of the yellow peril; and any number of other derogatory stereotypes for people of Asian origin.

My first instinct was to find any way that I could to blend in, be invisible, not stand out, to integrate and belong in my new community. But of course, I came to realize that I would *never* belong. That I would never fit in. And I learned very quickly that I would have to fight twice as hard, be twice as smart, and run twice as fast just to get half as far. These were invaluable lessons and were at the heart of why I eventually decided, later in life, to pursue the pathway of an entrepreneur — a pathway where my aspiration was deliberately *not* to fit in, but rather to create companies with purpose and vision that would challenge the status quo, and which others would be compelled to join — but only on my terms.

As someone who was not fortunate enough to be born here, I did not grow up with any sense of entitlement, nor did I have any expectation of life having to be "fair." *But that was my edge.* When one has nothing to lose and everything to gain, you don't waste a single opportunity, you take nothing for granted, and you value every sponsor and backer who takes a chance on you. It is a privilege to fight for your pathway forward because even the opportunity to fight for your beliefs and convictions was a privilege that did not exist at the time in my country of origin.

There is an unspoken bond between those who have shared this journey, and even though we may not know each other, we *recognize* each other as soon as we meet. It is a small club where the price of admission is hardship, but through that hardship comes tremendous rewards.

It comes as no surprise to me that over 50 percent of the most valuable companies in the world are founded by or led by immigrants and the sons and daughters of immigrants. That immigrant experience — of navigating new cultures, overcoming barriers, and continually striving to build a better life — parallels the entrepreneur's journey of breaking new ground, facing rejection, and relentlessly pursuing purpose and vision. These parallel tracks have instilled in me a resilience and a unique perspective on opportunity — seeing not just what was or is but always looking forward to what could be.

## THE FORMATIVE INFLUENCE OF WOMEN IN LEADERSHIP

Women have always been a cornerstone in my leadership evolution. My earliest memories as a young boy were formed after my mother and her young family (me and my younger sister) were sheltered by my grandmothers and my aunties after my father was forced to flee a military autocracy. My sister, Fay, was my constant companion and ended up being my business partner later in life through all of the companies that I founded or invested in.

When it comes to my career as an entrepreneur and a business leader, I can confirm that the saying about it being "lonely at the top" is completely true — especially for founders and entrepreneurs. We operate without safety nets, even at the best of times. You cherish and value that small circle of trusted advisers and colleagues who only have your interests at heart, who are willing to tell you things that no one else can or will, who are there to support you even through existential challenges and perfect storms.

In my life, none were more important than my wife and life partner, Katrina. She is the game changer for me and my chosen path, and I attribute all the success that I have been fortunate to experience to her being in my corner through my entire journey. The stamina to take on every challenge, the resilience to survive and thrive, my muse on the pulse of the generational changes that were taking place, the perspective to adapt to how the world and community work, my soft place to fall when navigating overwhelming challenge, and the special person with whom to share special life moments — all have only been possible because of the incredible support and unflinching belief that Katrina has had in me. I won the lottery when she came into my life.

Most entrepreneurs and successful business leaders whom I have spoken with have their own "Katrina," who has been the difference-maker in their journey. If you are fortunate enough to have that partner in your life, treasure them and never take them for granted. They are the key to unlocking the incredible rewards that come from your chosen pathway.

Reflecting on my journey, it's evident how women's perspectives have enriched my understanding of leadership. They've taught me the power of empathy, the strength in vulnerability, and the necessity of having diverse voices at the decision-making table. From all of them, I learned the power of inner strength, resilience, staying focused on the long game — and valuing the generosity of family, friends, and community.

## CONCLUSION

Throughout my journey, from the early days of struggling to find my footing in a new country to the rollercoaster ride of founding and building businesses, it's the connections with others that have fortified my resolve and fuelled my perseverance.

Human connection, in its essence, is the lifeblood of resilience. During the darkest days of my first company, when the aftermath of 9/11 threw us into turmoil, it was the strength of relationships that became our beacon of hope. It wasn't just about business strategies or market positioning; it was the genuine bonds we had formed with our team, our customers, and our partners that provided the foundation to withstand the storm. These connections weren't transactional; they were deeply personal, built on mutual respect, shared struggles, and collective ambitions.

Reflecting on those times, I'm reminded of the countless instances when a simple act of kindness from a colleague, a word of encouragement from a mentor, or even a shared laugh in the midst of chaos served as a reminder of why we push forward. It's these moments of connection that remind us that we're not alone in our journey, that our struggles are shared, and that our victories are multiplied.

Resilience is often seen as a solitary characteristic, a testament to individual strength. However, my experiences have taught me that resilience is profoundly communal. It's nurtured in the spaces between us, in the shared understanding that we are all navigating challenges, and in the commitment to support each other through them. The network of relationships that I've been fortunate enough to build has shown me time and again that the true measure of our resilience is not just in how we face adversity alone but in how we lift each other up, how we draw strength from our collective experiences, and how we emerge not just intact, but stronger together.

———

In conclusion, the importance of human connection to resilience is a theme that weaves through every chapter of my entrepreneurial story. It's a testament to the fact that while the path of innovation and business is often fraught with uncertainty and hardship, the connections we forge along the way are our most valuable asset. They remind us of our purpose, fuel our resilience, and ultimately, they are the reason we never f***ing quit.

**Yung Wu** is a serial entrepreneur, private equity investor, and experienced corporate director specializing in innovation, digital strategy, and technology. As the recently retired CEO of MaRS Discovery District, he led one of the world's largest innovation hubs, supporting over 1,200 companies employing over 30,000 tech workers in Canada's innovation economy. Under Yung's leadership, the MaRS innovation community grew by 450 percent over six years, contributing over $30 billion to Canada's GDP.

He co-founded the Coalition of Innovation Leaders Against Racism (CILAR) and derives great personal satisfaction from his philanthropic work with his wife, Katrina, through the MaRS Leadership Fund for climate innovation and their social enterprise "Different Is Cool."

# KEY FACTORS IN EFFECTIVE NETWORKING

### Shawn Allen | Founder of Matrix Mortgage Global

## CHOOSE DEPTH OVER BREADTH

I've always believed in nurturing deep connections rather than expanding a vast network. By choosing depth over breadth in networking, you're committing to fostering significant, mutually advantageous relationships instead of merely collecting a plethora of contacts. Take my bond with MLSE (Maple Leaf Sports & Entertainment), for instance. As a season ticket holder for both the Toronto Raptors and Toronto FC, I see immense value in the relationships I've cultivated over time. While some might argue that purchasing season tickets is an extravagant expense, the connections I've forged are priceless.

My courtside seats at Raptors games have afforded me two memorable trips with the team to Atlanta. During these trips, I've had the pleasure of meeting fellow season ticket holders. On my most recent journey, I crossed paths with a real estate developer — let's call him Jack. Jack, who hailed from my neck of the woods, was embroiled in a large-scale construction venture but faced hurdles in obtaining project approval. I suggested he attend the annual Mayor's Lunch I host. His interest piqued, Jack inquired, "Could I secure a seat near the mayor?" I assured him, "Become a platinum sponsor, and I'll place you right next to her."

This anecdote underscores how quality networking prioritizes enduring, trust-filled relationships. These relationships can culminate in sales, revenue, and stability, among other advantages. This method entails both contributing to and deriving benefits from your connections, building a robust core network of professionals who share your aspirations, and upholding relationships grounded in mutual support and trust. Although a broad network can offer widespread exposure, the focus on quality ties is universally acknowledged as the cornerstone of successful networking. The ultimate goal is to find a harmony that aligns with your professional ambitions and principles, acknowledging that the depth of your connections far outweighs their number.

## EMBRACE THE SPIRIT OF GIVING

Remember, networking is all about reciprocity. It's essential to enter into these relationships with the willingness to lend a hand and support those around you. Networking transcends the mere exchange of business cards — it's about forging real bonds and being there for one another. My ties with the University of Toronto Scarborough are a testament to this philosophy. I've had the privilege of organizing numerous prestigious networking events, and it's the students who reap the most rewards. They dive into deep conversations, feeling welcomed yet empowered by their unique student identities — their true superpower.

Keeping in touch and being a pillar of support not only strengthens your network but also underscores the importance of authenticity, sharing what you're passionate about, and uplifting others — these are the pillars of true networking. It's about nurturing a generous and expansive mindset, a continuous journey of aiding others in their path to success. In essence, effective networking is rooted in sincerity, providing support, and embracing a culture of generosity and personal development.

## NURTURING CONNECTIONS THROUGH FOLLOW-UP: A PERSONAL APPROACH

When it comes to relationship building, I firmly believe that timely follow-up is the secret sauce. Within one to two days of making new contacts, I make it a point to reach out. Why? Because this swift follow-up reinforces the initial connection, keeping the momentum alive. It's like tending to a freshly planted seed — you water it promptly to ensure growth.

So, what's my game plan for follow-up? First, I express genuine gratitude for the meeting. A simple "thank you for your time" goes a long way. Next, I recap our discussion, highlighting key points we covered. It's a subtle way of saying, "Hey, I was paying attention, and our chat mattered."

But here's the magic ingredient: purpose. I always follow up with a specific reason. Maybe I stumbled upon an article related to our conversation. Or perhaps I can offer assistance based on their interests. It's not about being pushy; it's about being relevant. By doing this, I keep the connection alive without overwhelming anyone.

Remember, networking isn't just about collecting business cards — it's about weaving a tapestry of relationships. And timely, purposeful follow-up threads that tapestry together, creating a network that's both strong and enduring.

## CARVING OUT TIME FOR CONNECTIONS: A PERSONAL NARRATIVE

I'm a firm believer in the power of face-to-face interactions, especially as we emerge from the shadow of COVID-19. Whether it's a business breakfast or a casual chat with my local bartender, I cherish these in-person meet-ups. Setting aside regular time for such interactions is the cornerstone of effective networking. It's about engaging in activities that foster and broaden your professional circle.

Connecting isn't an ad-hoc activity; it's a staple in my calendar. It's not about reaching out only when you need a favour; it's a sustained effort to support others on their road to success. Being consistently present is a testament to your dedication to your network. It's crucial for networking triumphs, allowing you to fine-tune your endeavours and extract maximum value from your time investment.

By adopting practical time-management tactics and earmarking specific periods for networking, you ensure that these efforts are given the attention they deserve. So, setting aside time for networking isn't just about expanding your professional contacts — it's about nurturing your career and paving the way for collective success.

## CRAFTING YOUR NETWORK WITH PURPOSE: A PERSONAL INSIGHT

Networking with intention is like navigating with a compass — it guides you to the right places, aligning with your personal and professional aspirations. I'm all about being choosy when it comes to the gatherings I attend and the circles I join. It's not about filling an address book; it's about connecting with the right crowd that complements my expertise and enriches my professional journey.

For me, it's about clarity and purpose. I ask myself, "Who do I want to meet? What do I aim to achieve?" before stepping into any event. This ensures my networking is not just a social dance but a strategic step towards my goals. And it's not a solo act — I'm there to contribute, to be a catalyst for others' success as much as my own.

From business mixers to industry conventions, from skill-building workshops to vibrant online forums, each venue is a choice made with intent. By networking with such deliberation, I don't just expand my circle — I enhance it, creating opportunities that correspond with my vision and values.

## CHOOSE YOUR NETWORKING SPACES WISELY

It's essential to be selective about the networking events and groups you join, ensuring they are in sync with your aspirations. I've always believed in the power of strategic networking. Back in 2018, I became a member of the Scarborough Business Association. It wasn't just about business; it was about planting roots in a community that mattered to me and my family. I sought to be an active voice in the conversations that sculpted our local business environment.

By being involved in the association, I've had the opportunity to forge meaningful relationships with other community organizations, developers, city councillors, and even members of federal and provincial Parliament. These relationships have strengthened my roots in the community, allowing me to contribute more effectively and align my goals with the collective vision.

This method is all about fostering meaningful connections rather than accumulating contacts. It's about understanding who you want to meet and why, setting clear objectives for each interaction, and ensuring every handshake aligns with your end goals. Being intentional in networking also means contributing to others' success as much as you seek your own growth.

By choosing your networking arenas with intention — from industry-specific forums and professional development sessions to online communities — you not only enrich your professional circle but also open doors to more substantial, unique, and relevant opportunities that support your journey.

## REMEMBER, EVERYONE HOLDS A TREASURE WITHIN

Embracing the belief that each person you meet has something valuable to share is essential to forging genuine professional bonds. It's about seeing the potential in every interaction, whether it's a chat with the doorman at your favourite restaurant, a brief encounter with an usher at a concert, or an engaging conversation with your Uber driver en route to your destination.

This philosophy is rooted in the idea of mutual enrichment — it's about what you can offer, not just what you can gain. It's a mindset of generosity and personal growth, a continuous journey of empowering others to succeed. Everyone possesses unique gifts — be it knowledge, skills, time, or connections — and it's up to us to harness these gifts to uplift those around us.

By adopting this approach, we lay the foundation for relationships built on trust and reciprocal support, weaving a network that's not only robust but invaluable. Recognizing the inherent worth in each person and dedicating yourself to their advancement is a transformative networking strategy, one that paves the way for relationships that are both rewarding and rich with opportunity.

## BE PREPARED

When preparing for networking, it is essential to schedule appointments and be ready to present yourself well. This involves setting clear goals for the event, doing your homework about the attendees and the event itself, and having a well-polished elevator pitch. Additionally, it's important to dress professionally, have business cards or resumes ready, and be equipped to communicate your strengths and what you can bring to the table. Being prepared allows you to make the most of your time at the event and present yourself in a confident and professional manner. It also includes following up with new contacts after the event to continue building those relationships. Doing all this will maximize the opportunities that networking events offer and make meaningful relationships that align with your personal or professional goals.

In the realm of networking, I've come to realize the importance of connecting with individuals who have the potential to significantly influence my career and help me achieve my goals. It's a strategy that goes beyond the superficial exchange of contact information. Imagine a vast Rolodex brimming with potential, each name a seed that, when nurtured, can grow into a fruitful relationship. This approach is not about tallying up favours; it's about the authentic desire to contribute to others' success.

The true power of your network lies in its ability to elevate your career, enhance your self-confidence, and open doors to new opportunities. It's about forming connections that are as much about giving as receiving. Advice, introductions, and shared ideas become the currency of a rich network.

Engagement is key. By actively participating in conversations, offering insights, and showing up — whether online or in person — you keep the network dynamic alive. It's akin to cultivating a garden; with regular attention and care, it flourishes.

Networking with intention means seeking out those who can truly make a difference in your life. It's about creating a ripple effect with each genuine interaction, shaping your professional journey in profound and unexpected ways.

------

Networking is a continuous journey, not just a series of one-off meetings. It's about cultivating lasting relationships that persist long after you've secured a job. For me, it's the personal touches that count, like remembering birthdays. A call on someone's special day can warm their heart more than any text or email — it's a gesture that shows you truly care.

But networking is more than just remembering dates; it's about nurturing relationships. Being proactive in reaching out, starting conversations, and seeking advice shows that you're genuinely interested in others' paths.

Staying active in your network is crucial. Engaging with others' content, sharing valuable insights, and being present in conversations are all ways to show you're invested. It's about being a familiar presence, much like a regular at a café who's always noticed.

Organizing your contacts and setting reminders to catch up ensures that you maintain these relationships. Whether it's a casual coffee chat, sharing industry insights, or lending a hand, consistency is key.

Utilizing various communication tools — emails, phone calls, social media, and in-person meetings — helps keep these relationships vibrant. Each mode of communication adds a unique tone to the symphony of your network.

Attending events, whether they're online webinars, industry conferences, or local meet-ups, is also essential. They're opportunities to meet new people and maintain existing connections, fostering a network that's not just a fallback but a springboard for growth and new possibilities.

———

In summary, effective relationship building goes beyond mere introductions; it focuses on developing substantial connections that encourage shared advancement and collaboration. Prioritizing meaningful interactions allows individuals to create a network that is more beneficial than a broad but shallow one. Adopting a mindset of generosity fosters an environment where assistance is mutual, enhancing the overall experience for everyone involved.

Active involvement in discussions and remembering personal details about your contacts can elevate a fleeting encounter into a lasting partnership. Utilizing diverse communication methods keeps your connections lively and engaging, while participating in relevant events consistently opens avenues for new possibilities. Ultimately, the journey of building a strong network relies on sincerity, kindness, and a commitment to nurturing relationships over time. By embracing these strategies, you can create a robust network that not only advances your career goals but also enriches your life.

**Shawn Allen,** a prominent figure in Canadian finance, epitomizes the essence of Scarborough, having been born, raised, and currently residing in this vibrant community. In 2008, he founded Matrix Mortgage Global, guiding it to become the premier private lending brokerage in the nation. Empathizing with barriers to higher education, he established the University of Toronto Shawn Allen Award scholarship for students in the Faculty of Management and International Business. This initiative underscores his dedication to both the finance industry and the betterment of his community.

# INVITE OTHERS TO THE TABLE AND ASK YOURSELF, "WHAT'S STOPPING YOU?"

### Mitzie Hunter | President and CEO of the Canadian Women's Foundation

### SAYING YES WHEN INVITED

Look around the room. I mean really look. Who's there? Who's missing? This is what you must do every time you enter a room. Because if we want real inclusion, we must first begin by noticing who's not there. Notice who's missing and invite them in.

———

David Tsubouchi became an MPP and cabinet minister during the time I was finishing my undergraduate studies at University of Toronto Scarborough. The immigrant communities in Scarborough, where I am from, took note. Seeing diverse people in leadership is relevant and an important inspiration for young people.

Some years later, when I was just starting out in my career as an executive and civic leader, I met another David who was to have a major impact on my life: David Pecaut. On the surface, David was a most unlikely advocate for a young professional Black woman from Scarborough. He was a white, midwestern U.S.–raised male, close to twenty years my senior, who, as senior partner and managing director of Boston Consulting Group, was responsible for launching countless city-building projects in his adopted city. As a result, he was well connected to the power brokers in the City of Toronto. David knew and understood the value of "seeing" others who might be on the fringes of that inner circle and inviting them to the table. He saw me, invited me in, and quickly became my friend and mentor. That's what he did for me. It may sound like something small, but it was huge. He first invited me to join the Toronto City Summit Alliance (which later became the Greater Toronto CivicAction Alliance), where he was chair. Then, once I was at the table, he continued to urge me to take on various leadership roles within the organization.

———

Let's start with how I got to the room in the first place. It wasn't unusual for me to enter rooms and be the only Black woman or person of colour. Too often, I was the only woman of any colour. That was the reality of being the president of a technology business association. I could attend whole conferences or show up at business networking lunches and be among just a handful of women and the only Black woman.

In the early 2000s, I was president of a technology incubator called SMART Toronto. I was out there in the tech space and start-up community, navigating the choppy waters of the dot-com boom and bust. It was a roller coaster with thrilling heights and deep depths.

Toronto and many regions across Canada, such as Ottawa, Waterloo, Vancouver, and Halifax, were — and still are — thriving spaces for Canada's tech start-ups. SMART Toronto, an association for the tech community, was leading the technology conversation among start-ups, hardware, software, new media and telecommunications companies, and governments. This was my first big leadership job, and I loved it. It was a wild ride. I had so much fun and met so many awesome people working in this fast-paced, pulsing space where everything was measured in web years.

I believe the coming together of people to do great and extraordinary things is what builds community. Connections matter in large cities just as much as they give small towns their charm and character. I have always relished being a part of building connections, and I've always wanted to do big, bold things with my life.

————

In 2002, I was part of the coming together of an extraordinary group of people. I was formally invited to an exclusive meeting and call to service of business and community leaders to talk about Toronto and how to make it better. I was surprised initially by the invitation as it was clear that I was being included because of the position I held as president of SMART Toronto. It was so unique to be asked to join this broad yet exclusive group of leaders, and I was curious to see what the meeting would be about. So, I decided to accept and show up.

The meeting was held at the University of Toronto's Rotman School of Management building at 105 St. George Street in Toronto. As I walked into the room, I could sense that something big and important was going to happen. I quickly scanned the room and found a spot near the back of the room.

The first keynote speaker was just getting started. David Pecaut gave an unforgettable talk entitled "Why I Love Toronto." As I watched his well-polished presentation, I was enraptured by what he said. He loved this city, and he wasn't afraid to use powerful words when expressing his passion for it. He saw the city's potential through the uniqueness of the people, their diverse perspectives, their skills and talent. David went to great lengths to live in Toronto, even commuting each week from his offices in New York City, spending three days in Toronto and four days in New York. He saw that the potential of this city was limitless. The beauty of our neighbourhoods. The diversity of our people. The limitless potential to innovate.

He echoed my sentiments precisely. I, too, *loved* Toronto. It was my chosen place. It was a city into which I wanted to invest my time and

Invite Others to the Table and Ask Yourself, "What's Stopping You?" | 185 talents and help reimagine how the future could be. I wanted to roll up my sleeves and get to work. In fact, I had been doing just that starting from a young age, carrying forward into my workplaces and community.

At the conclusion of the meeting, a broad invitation was thrown out by the Toronto City Summit Alliance chairs, Frances Lankin (former MPP and then president and CEO of United Way), David Crombie (former mayor of Toronto and CEO of the Canadian Urban Institute) and John Tory (soon to throw his hat in the ring in the Toronto mayoral race). They urged those in the room to stay involved and help solve the city's challenges. I was eager to participate in building an even greater city, so I quickly put my name on the list and waited. To my surprise, I never got a call.

I reached out to the organizers but was told I hadn't been assigned a role. I wondered about this. How could it be that an organization so eager to receive contributions of ideas from leaders across the city, whose vision to create a better city so aligned with mine, had left me out? I could only conclude it was because I was unknown to the organizers. I was outside of the inner circle.

I later saw David Pecaut, and he asked me why I wasn't at the meetings to action the ideas that emerged from the summit. I said I wasn't given an opportunity to join. David asked, "Who told you that?" He felt deeply that we needed everyone to be part of the solution. With that endorsement, I jumped in enthusiastically.

Subsequently, Toronto went through the SARS epidemic. The city was slow to recover from its ravaging effects and needed a boost. It was up to those in leadership to do something about it. Seeing that the Toronto City Summit Alliance was already in place, the city turned to its leadership for help. David Pecaut and hundreds of other leaders stepped forward to meet the challenge. I watched as plans were put in place for a huge concert at Downsview Park with the Rolling Stones!

## STAY AT THE TABLE

A couple of years later, I had changed jobs and left the tech sector and my president role; I stopped attending the meetings. I again ran into David, who was now chair of the alliance, and he asked where I was and why I had stopped coming to the meetings. Once again, he had noticed I was missing from the conversation. He once again pointed out, "Mitzie, we need you. We need your voice and your unique perspectives. Our table is not complete without you." I told David I had moved from the tech sector to a non-profit charitable space at Goodwill Industries. David was adamant. "The table isn't complete without your voice. You bring a view that we don't have, and we need you there even more now that you are in the charitable sector."

With that, I became even more involved in every aspect of the Toronto City Summit Alliance. I co-chaired the Emerging Leaders Network with Donna Lindell, a former corporate communications executive. We brought together young, civic-minded people to reimagine a better city. I stayed at the table. I attended every city summit. I took part in various working groups and was involved in report writing for important city-building initiatives such as MISWAA (Modernizing Income Security for Working-Age Adults), Enough Talk — An Action Plan for the Toronto Region, and Greening Greater Toronto. I witnessed and enjoyed the birth of Luminato, a global arts festival; TRIEC (the Toronto Region Immigrant Employment Council); and the Diversity Fellows, a program that is accelerating the next generation of civic leaders. I volunteered enthusiastically for ten years before eventually becoming the CEO of the Toronto City Summit Alliance's successor, CivicAction.

At CivicAction, I was able to lead the formation of the Transportation Champions Council, which helped to encourage needed investment in transit for Metrolinx's transportation plan, the Big Move. I provided support for the Green Canada Fund advisory board. I triggered the transformation of the Greater Toronto Marketing Alliance into Toronto Global, an entity that is now attracting global companies to invest in the Toronto region. I established the WeatherWise Partnership to make our cities more climate resilient through adaptation measures. All of this was accomplished because the door was now open. More importantly, when I found that door closed, I knocked and kept knocking until I was let in.

This early experience was formative for me. I always remembered the advice of David Pecaut about paying attention to who's in the room and, perhaps more importantly, who isn't. Be an inclusive leader and invite others in. Leave space for youth, for retirees, for people with lived experiences, for diverse people, and for people of all income levels, languages, and voices. In doing so, you will find that everyone you connect with will have something of value to contribute. Something that, coming out of their own unique experience and perspective, will have been overlooked or not even imagined were they not part of that discussion. When all people are given opportunities to be involved in community building, amazing things can happen.

———

I kept running into David as I was out and about in Toronto. The last time we spoke before he passed away was on Bay Street, in front of the former Ben McNally's bookstore location. We had both attended a book launch and were leaving at the same time. He told me he was on his way home to make a salad; he said it was going to be a very big salad. He then gave me some advice that evening that has stayed with me: "What I've learned is that you must eat way more greens than you think you should." I remember his smile before he walked up Bay Street into the glow of the evening sun. David's final words meant that I should look after myself.

Later when I became a politician, I would encourage my teams to do the same. Eat your greens. Invite others to the table, especially those who are missing. The life lessons that I learned from David Pecaut and many others throughout my life and varied career paths have been invaluable to me.

188 | The Ripple Effect

## TAKING BOLD STEPS

I have benefited from many women who have supported my career and life choices. They have been my role models, bosses, mentors, coaches, sponsors, and champions. Often, they saw my potential before I had realized it. When someone else believes in you, it gives you the courage to find your way forward.

Many of these woman mentors and role models continue to inspire and empower me. Among them is Dr. Jean Augustine, the first Black woman elected to the Parliament of Canada. Dr. Augustine has always made time to mentor others. When I was a manager at Bell, I went to see her in her office in Etobicoke-Lakeshore. As I was about to leave, she asked me to sit back down. She gave me powerful advice. She said, "Be ready whenever you get the call." This motivated me to go back to school and get an MBA. Investing in yourself and lifelong learning is something I wholeheartedly believe in.

For women, networking can be a powerful force in the workplace and the community.

Early in my career, I became a member of Verity Club, and through the many executive women that I met, my aspirations for leadership were sharpened. I recall being part of a MasterMIND session led by Jacqui d'Eon, former chief communications officer at Deloitte Consulting, with other women leaders who supported me and challenged me about fulfilling my life's purpose, which could include elected office and other leadership roles.

Often, when other people validate and reflect who you are and who you could be, it opens a door, instills confidence, and gives you the courage you need to step forward undaunted.

When I expressed my desire to get into politics, my MasterMIND group, with Jacqui at the helm, simply asked, "What's stopping you?" It was a profound moment. When I thought about it, nothing. I knew I could take this bold step at the right time.

For me, that time came a few years later when I got the call to run for elected office from Ontario's first woman premier, Kathleen

Wynne. Kathleen knew me from my various civic roles at Goodwill and CivicAction. As CEO of CivicAction, I had been invited to her government's first Speech from the Throne (which sets out the government's goals at the beginning of each new parliamentary session). I sat in the gallery in the Ontario Legislative Chamber and listened. I believed in the work she wanted to do for Ontarians. After meeting separately with Deborah Matthews, who was deputy premier and minister of health, and Yasir Naqvi, a cabinet minister, I knew I would find my place on the Ontario Liberal team and be able to make a difference for my community. Kathleen wanted me on her team, and I quickly said yes.

I was excited to have the chance to represent my community in Scarborough. It didn't take me long to make this decision because I already knew I wanted to enter politics. The seeds for public service had been planted and were strongly rooted by this time. I decided to run in the 2013 by-election, putting my job as CEO of CivicAction on hold.

———

The first seed was planted early, when I was a student leader in high school and president of my students' council. It was later nurtured by Jean Augustine, who saw something in me and encouraged me to be ready. I finally got the chance to hone my skills when given civic leadership roles as part of CivicAction. I was prompted to thrive and grow as part of a women-led MasterMIND group at Verity, who, within a safe space, challenged me to answer that critical question, "What's stopping you?"

This core question can be applied to any opportunity you are contemplating. When you stop to think about it, the answer is often this: nothing. Throwing aside any fears or doubts, you can make the decision to go for it. Be bold in taking that step in your life's journey.

So many times, I meet women and men who tell me I have helped them in their careers or community work. I may have recommended them for a board position, and they are now leaders serving on corporate boards. I might have shared my leadership journey, showing up even after someone tried to block my progress. People find inspiration in the successes *and* the difficult times. One young man told me I had challenged him to become involved in making changes in his community. This encouragement gives them the courage to persevere and realize their boldest dreams.

Whenever I give talks to students, I tell them about loving what you do so much that you would do it for free. Imagine getting paid to do what you love. I had that chance in some of the roles I held, including president of SMART Toronto and CEO of CivicAction. For both of these leadership positions, I spent years volunteering, which led to full-time commitments.

Mostly, young people tell me how important it is for them to see someone in leadership who looks like them. Essentially, it allows them to imagine themselves in these roles, follow their dreams, and reach their full potential. David Tsubouchi might not have realized it, but seeing him in leadership all those years ago helped me to know that I could do it, too.

Here is my bold list to get what you want out of life and have an impact:

1. Show up.
2. Don't count yourself out.
3. Do what you love with people who love you back.
4. When you have a big life decision to make, ask yourself, what's stopping you? Go for it!

**Mitzie Hunter** has a proven track record of building and championing the City of Toronto and its residents, having served as the MPP for Scarborough-Guildwood, securing four consecutive election victories over the course of a decade. Her thirty years of leadership extends to several high-level positions, including roles in the provincial cabinet where she served as Minister of Education, Minister of Advanced Education and Skills Development, and Associate Minister of Finance, entrusted with overseeing the Ontario Retirement Pension Plan. She is currently the president and CEO of the Canadian Women's Foundation, a public foundation for gender justice and equality.

# WHAT IS THE ENDGAME OF NETWORKING? REDISCOVERING THE VALUE OF HUMAN CONNECTION

### Krishan Mehta, PhD | Vice-President of University Advancement and Alumni Relations at Toronto Metropolitan University

Almost thirty years ago, renowned sociologist Manuel Castells wrote a groundbreaking book called *The Rise of the Network Society*, in which he explored the growing value of technology in building networks of people and communities across borders and cultures. He, along with a number of other prominent writers from that time, propelled an exciting field of study focused on the critical importance of networks in all aspects of modern life. And it certainly caught on like wildfire; students and academics alike widely used network theory as a way to make sense of their own research, especially as people started to depend on their devices to connect, communicate, and collaborate on just about everything. Who would have imagined that just three decades later, technology would become the primary vehicle to find community and belonging? It appears that Marshall McLuhan was onto something.

As a recovering doctoral student in the field of philanthropy, I find great value in thinking about the role of networks — sometimes glibly referred to as "the Rolodex" — in helping to advance charitable causes. After all, the adage "it's not what you know, it's who you know" is often applied to mainstream fundraising practice. Another rampant cliché: Fundraising is all about relationships. Entering my twenty-fifth year as a fundraising professional in Toronto, I occasionally return to these concepts as a way to make better sense of my experiences with donors, colleagues, and volunteers. Is networking inherently critical to fundraising success? How has networking changed, especially in a post-pandemic world? How can networking help you break in or, better yet, break through when you are new to the scene? Ultimately, for me, all these questions roll up into one meta-query: Is human connection the endgame to networking?

## REVISITING THE COCKTAIL RECEPTION

To explore this question, let's take a bird's-eye view of a scene we are all too familiar with, the charity gala — a networker's ultimate playground. It starts with a cocktail hour in the reception hall. People jam into a small space as the bar lineup grows longer, cutting the room in half. Guests squeeze by one another, moving with great purpose towards servers holding coveted trays of canapés. You scan the room in search of someone you may know. Once welcomed into a circle, small talk ensues — "Traffic was a nightmare." "Summer is around the corner." "Tonight's keynote is supposed to be great." Suggested attire: business. Of course, this isn't just a charity world phenomenon. Business lunches, academic conferences, membership club meetings, professional after-hours events, weddings, funerals, you name it — all have this sort of networking component attached to them.

And while few would fully dismiss the value of the networking get-together, I sometimes wonder if it is a meaningful catalyst for establishing true, reciprocal relationships. After all, you now have their business card and, just for that, it was a successful venture. Or was it?

After years of researching and exploring various theories about networking, community building, and belonging, I can't help but see these moments as interactions between two distinct groups: the networkers and the already-networked. To put it plainly: The former are often there to meet "net-new" people, while the latter don't really need to network at all. Networkers show up for a defined purpose: to grow their contacts, to source new donors, to find a new job, or to establish camaraderie with people of similar backgrounds.

The networked, on the other hand, have a different purpose — to reconnect with well-established contacts, to advance a personal or professional relationship, or, dare I say, to be seen in the right room with the right people for the right cause. Social scientists would look at the interactions between the networker and the networked as expressions of how class, power, and privilege function in our society. Going back to the cocktail reception then, the difference between the two groups can be palpable: The networked are standing still in the reception hall, often holding court and surrounded by people waiting to say hello. The networkers, on the other hand, are working the room — buzzing around, exchanging cards, and shaking hands with everyone.

I wish I could confidently say that people go to charity events solely to help raise awareness and funds for a worthwhile cause. But the truth of the matter is that most are there for a dual purpose: to do something good and to be in the company of one another — to network. Admittedly, when it comes down to it, the latter will often trump the former. That's the power and potency of networking.

## POSING AS ONE OF THE NETWORKED: A SOCIAL EXPERIMENT

Over the last few months, as I was thinking more about the networker-networked paradigm, I decided to see what would happen if I dropped my networker identity to play the role of a networked person at a few upcoming fundraising events and gatherings. What would occur if I went into a space not caring about who I needed to meet, rather just being present and taking in whatever and whoever came to me? Would the outcome be any different than the thousands of times I went in to work the room? At some of these events, I was known to a healthy number of people, while at others, I knew one or two at most. Placing myself in a good location in a room, I would stand, smiling at passersby, waiting for that moment of connection. I deliberately decided to move slowly and intentionally through the space. I went into this experiment thinking I would have limited success; after all, I didn't possess any material gravitational force (I wasn't a major donor prospect or influencer) and, quite frankly, it didn't really matter if I was there or not — the show would certainly go on without me. Delving into my methodology and various observations would take up far too many pages, so allow me to share several top-line lessons from this experiment.

Networked people have deeper conversations: How many times have you been in front of that person who is scanning the room past your shoulder? How many times have you caught yourself distracted by the who-else-is-here effect? Over the last few months, as a networked person, I was surprised by the number of meaningful discussions I entered into with people I knew casually or even sometimes with perfect strangers. Holding attention to the person in front of me, I wasn't going to let a passerby distract us from conversations about a wide range of deeper-level issues, from personal health challenges to feelings of belonging at work and anxiety about world events. As a networked person, I learned something meaningful from my interactions, and I felt a sense of ease that I didn't need to work the room — having just a few deep conversations was quite gratifying and powerful enough.

Time moves slower when you aren't the networker; networking shouldn't be a race against the clock. It takes time to establish a connection, deepen your knowledge, and learn something new. By having fewer one-on-one or one-on-two conversations lasting anywhere from ten to twenty minutes, I found that a networking hour gently sailed by with very little wind pushing time forward. With over two decades of participating in (and leading) events, I know that a networker's gold medal is often achieved by counting the number of touchpoints made by the end of a gathering. In the world of networking, we often reward quantity over quality. Consequently, conversations and connections are rushed, unfulfilling, and, more often than not, forgettable.

Networkers work hard at working the room: Fundraisers are often sent into networking environments by their organizations to raise awareness and even develop new prospects. It's a major investment of money and time, especially for smaller charities with limited resources. In my new networked persona, I rarely left events and meetings mentally or physically exhausted, unlike the countless times when I was the networker. Few people would peg me as an introvert, but I have found ways to replenish energy spent in social settings. Introverts get a bad rep for being overly protective of their energy, often running in the other direction when asked to attend a networking function. At large events, introverted fundraisers can behave more like the networked, focusing on just one or two deep interactions. In the end, those of us in the charity world understand this is the ideal way to build a lasting connection, not by tussling one's way through crowds in an effort to strike deals.

The search for belonging can be rough. I find it surprising that in a large city like Toronto, I can still be one of the only racialized people at a fundraising or networking event. On more than one occasion, I — as a networker — have been asked, "Where is the coat check?" Or "I'll have a glass of red" from a guest who thought I was the wait staff when it was clear to others that I was there for another purpose. While racial bias can certainly make an unexpected appearance within and beyond the networking sphere, what is perhaps more harmful is the impact it has on one's sense of belonging within a community. Interestingly, when I am networking in diverse spaces, not once have I ever felt that I was an outsider or didn't belong there. Introductory conversations — especially during my experiment as a networked person — seemed to last a little longer and go much deeper. "Tell me more about that experience at work" or "How are you coping with that situation at home?" As a racialized networked person, I also noticed that other people of colour wanted to connect, perhaps with a knowing glance that there was a solidarizing experience to be had.

It's possible to leave the business cards at home; you don't have to dive into a jacket pocket to offer your contact information. Observing the networked closely, they are judicious about who they keep in touch with after a social engagement. Over the last few months, I gave out fewer business cards but found that I wasn't any worse off. If people really wanted to connect with me (or if I wanted to keep the conversation going), we have LinkedIn and search engines to be able to find one another. I would imagine that many of us have a stack of business cards on our desks but, months later, struggle to put names and faces together. Truthfully, it's difficult for me sometimes to even remember when and where that connection was made! I am not suggesting that the card exchange ritual is futile, but there is merit in being purposeful about it. And if you legitimately forgot your business cards, there are a number of apps that can easily ensure that new contacts go directly into your phone. In recent months, for example, I have used QR codes to share and load contacts into my digital address book.

Small talk is making a comeback. Stemming from various pandemic lockdowns, we have been conditioned to jump into the deep end with our virtual conversations, getting right down to business. Zoom social hours have mostly evaporated as everyone's schedules, responsibilities, and interests in virtual connectivity have changed, especially as we settle into a new hybrid reality. Since late 2023, however, I have observed a slow re-emergence of an appetite for in-person networking, as online meetings, while efficient, will never have the same impact as face-to-face interactions. Posing as the networked person, I had the chance to probe into this theme many times with networkers, and I heard repeatedly how critical it was to actually see people in the flesh, in real-time. As one person said, "Networking is meant to be a tactile experience — it's not only an exchange of words that matter but also the nuanced experience of sharing emotions, stories, and care for the person in front of you." In the end, it appears as though in-person networking will always be the tried-and-true winner in the pursuit of deep human connectivity.

———

So, is human connection the endgame to networking? I propose that networking is the spark for enduring human connection. Whether your motivations are rooted in professional or personal growth, entering a networking environment is, at its core, meant to be a fulfilling experience so long as it's inspired by purpose and intention. As the networkers and the networked exchange ideas and find common ground, it is important to remember that intrinsic to us all is the desire to belong, demonstrate reciprocity, and build trusting relationships. As a fundraiser, I believe the building and sharing of a network can make way for extraordinary expressions of generosity. It's the cornerstone of good philanthropy.

**Dr. Krishan Mehta** is the vice-president of advancement at Toronto Metropolitan University, where he leads philanthropy, alumni relations, fundraising campaigns, and other strategies in support of the university. Previously, he held a variety of fundraising and marketing roles at Seneca Polytechnic and the University of Toronto. Krishan also heads up the Fundraising Management Program at the G. Raymond Chang School of Continuing Education and teaches in Carleton University's Philanthropy and Non-Profit Leadership Graduate Program. Krishan has a PhD, and his research focuses on immigrant and diaspora philanthropy. He serves on the board of the Canadian Council for the Advancement of Education and is a frequent speaker on emerging issues in the charitable sector. Krishan has received several national and global accolades for his philanthropy leadership and contributions to fundraising education.

# THE FINAL WORD:
# THE RIPPLE EFFECT OF NETWORKING

### David Tsubouchi & Marc Kealey

Two things about which, as co-editors, we would agree: One is that this book reflects on how important it is to network and, of course, how that skill can help people to win in business, in politics, and in life. The other is more on the process of networking.

There are many chapters in our book on how to go through the process of creating a strategy to network effectively. Some contributors have highlighted how they achieved success through networking — meeting professionals from various levels of organizations. Networking, they point out, is important as one never knows what type of opportunity is out there, and it can help build confidence.

Effective business, political, and social networking makes one more confident because making connections with others develops social skills that can be advantageous to career advancement or gaining prominence. Being able to talk to anyone, no matter their position, can help in developing communication skills that lead to greater business, political, and social effectiveness.

There are many common threads that run through the stories of our friends. Those who have contributed to this book are people who are highly successful in the public and private sectors and, for the most part, started from very humble backgrounds. One can point to any of them and think they are great examples of perseverance and that by being good, decent people, they have done well. Has it been easy? Perhaps not, but we believe that if they could do it, so could you.

*The Ripple Effect* is a collection of stories on effectively using a network to create a benefit. In other words, in networking, behaviours influence not only our immediate colleagues but also individuals who are part of an even larger network, creating the ripple effect. The lessons are instructive, and the contributing writers in this book represent Canada perfectly — they are Indigenous, Asian, Black, immigrants, women, and men. Their messages are simple, distinct, and clear: Be confident in what you have to offer when meeting new business connections.

Some instructions are even more practical — make physical and mental lists of established business networks so that you are able to offer others your contacts as well. Networking is a two-way street, so always make sure you know what contacts might be helpful in different situations. Not only can networking lead to friends, but friends can also lead to networking.

Our book aspires to outline that networking can become the most important skill you'll ever cultivate. It is an essential craft to master, no matter what industry you work in or your level of experience. Good networking forms a basis of trust and support — and that can provide the opportunity to build mutually beneficial relationships with other professionals.

Having the right contacts in your professional network can help maximize opportunities. Networking is about sharing, not taking. It is about forming trust and helping each other towards goals — whatever they are. Regularly engaging with your contacts and finding opportunities to assist them helps to strengthen any relationship. By doing this, you sow the seeds for reciprocal assistance when you may need help to achieve your own goals.

By continually putting yourself out there and meeting new people, you're effectively stepping outside your comfort zone and building invaluable skills and self-confidence that you can take with you anywhere. The more you network, the more you'll grow and the more you will develop lasting connections.

Of course, the point of networking is to develop and nurture professional relationships, but some of the strongest and most long-standing friendships are born from business or political connections. Networking contacts are probably like-minded people with similar goals, so it's likely that a professional network will spill over into personal friendships. Be open to people who are already in your life or perhaps who you might meet at a social or political event as potential business contacts. You never know where your next great connection might come from, so the lessons herein are that we should pay close attention to those already in our lives.

Most importantly, the essence of good networking is about having the courage to go beyond your area of specialty. One of the most lacking traits in society is curiosity — be curious! Persevere! But above all, enjoy the experience and the moment.

We hope this book will be part of your journey to attain your goals. Networking results in good karma, and when done effectively and with integrity, it truly has a ripple effect.

**Entertainment. Writing. Culture.** ─────────────────────

ECW is a proudly independent, Canadian-owned book publisher. We know great writing can improve people's lives, and we're passionate about sharing original, exciting, and insightful writing across genres.

──────────────────────────── **Thanks for reading along!**

We want our books not just to sustain our imaginations, but to help construct a healthier, more just world, and so we've become a certified B Corporation, meaning we meet a high standard of social and environmental responsibility — and we're going to keep aiming higher. We believe books can drive change, but the way we make them can too.

Being a B Corp means that the act of publishing this book should be a force for good — for the planet, for our communities, and for the people that worked to make this book. For example, everyone who worked on this book was paid at least a living wage. You can learn more at the Ontario Living Wage Network.

This book is also available as a Global Certified Accessible™ (GCA) ebook. ECW Press's ebooks are screen reader friendly and are built to meet the needs of those who are unable to read standard print due to blindness, low vision, dyslexia, or a physical disability.

This book is printed on FSC®-certified paper. It contains recycled materials, and other controlled sources, is processed chlorine free, and is manufactured using biogas energy.

ECW's office is situated on land that was the traditional territory of many nations, including the Wendat, the Anishinaabeg, Haudenosaunee, Chippewa, Métis, and current treaty holders the Mississaugas of the Credit. In the 1880s, the land was developed as part of a growing community around St. Matthew's Anglican and other churches. Starting in the 1950s, our neighbourhood was transformed by immigrants fleeing the Vietnam War and Chinese Canadians dispossessed by the building of Nathan Phillips Square and the subsequent rise in real estate value in other Chinatowns. We are grateful to those who cared for the land before us and are proud to be working amidst this mix of cultures.

ecwpress.com